A Down-to-Earth Energy Book

547

T I P S

FOR

$AVING ENERGY

IN YOUR HOME

ROGER ALBRIGHT

Storey Communications, Inc.
Schoolhouse Road
Pownal, Vermont 05261

Cover and text design by Carol Jessop

Printed in the United States by Courier

Albright, Roger, 1922-
    547 Tips for saving energy in your home / by Roger Albright. — Rev. ed.
        p.   cm. — (A Down-to-earth energy book)
    ISBN 0-88266-677-0 (pbk.)
    1. Dwellings—Energy conservation. I. Title. II. Series.
TJ163.5.D86A43   1990
644—dc20   90-15491
                                                  CIP

CONTENTS

─── INTRODUCTION ───

We learned in the 1970s that the United States was extremely dependent on imported foreign oil for use in our businesses, industries, and homes. This lesson is being relearned today. We also now know that energy conservation is an important and effective way to reduce global warming and acid rain, and increase the quality of the air we breathe.

We can be more comfortable and increase our standard of living through investments in energy conservation. This book will provide information and guidance on some practical and affordable things you can do to your home and in your daily life to save energy.

First, a quick lesson on how your home loses heat.

➡ **Conduction:** Hold a glass in your hand. Fill the glass with hot water. The outer surface of the glass feels warm. Heat is transferred from the water to your hand through the glass by conduction. So long as the water is warmer than your hand, heat will conduct through the glass. Nothing actually passes through the glass; instead, fast-moving molecules bump against their neighbors, making them heat up. In the same way, heat passes through walls.

A material which slows down the flow of heat can be used as insulation. Most insulation materials work in basically the same way. They trap air in tiny pockets and prevent air currents from quickly taking the heat away.

The ability of a material to stop heat flow and act as insulation is called its "R-factor." The higher the R-factor, the better the insulation. When buying insulation, always look for the highest R-factor. There are other factors that you must also consider in choosing insulation: cost, ease of installation, durability, flammability, and water resistance.

➡ **Convection:** Hold a stick of incense next to a cold window. Which way does the smoke go? Down. Hold it next to a warm radiator. The smoke rises. The smoke is riding on currents of air. Because cold air falls, near a chilly window air currents go downward. Conversely, near a radiator air rises. Air currents carry heat from one place to another.

On windy days, a thin film of air surrounding our bodies is swept away by the wind. We lose heat. Our bodies heat another layer of air. Again, it is swept away. This is commonly known as the "windchill factor".

Homes also lose heat through convection. Heated air constantly rises inside your home and is swept away through holes or cracks. Cold air enters, especially near the floor. Convection in the home is often felt as a draft.

➡ **Radiation:** Do you feel cold when you stand next to a large picture window on a cold winter day? Does your front feel warm and your back feel cold when you stand in front of the wood stove? In each case, radiation is at work. Warm surfaces radiate or lose their heat to cold surfaces. You are radiating your heat to that cold window. The woodstove radiates its heat to the room. Radiators work through radiation and convection. The surface area radiates heat and air currents carry it into the room.

We will be using these concepts as we guide you through ways to save energy. It is helpful to know *how* heat energy is transferred when you're trying to reduce heat loss.

Note. In the chapters on home weatherization, we speak mostly about heating. If you live in a region where it is hot in the winter and even hotter in the summer, these same practices will help you save on your cooling bill. Chapter 3 and a section of Chapter 12 focus on cooling.

Our Home is a System

Over the past twenty years, we have learned that the house is a system. If you do something to one area, you will probably affect another area. That's why we need to consider humidity, moisture, and air quality when we are contemplating energy improvements.

We will point out how these systems interact as we discuss each topic. For example, condensation relates to the degree of insulation. Warm air can hold a lot of moisture. When the air cools down, it can hold less moisture. Just think about those hot, humid summer days. Have you ever noticed water dripping down the outside of a cold glass of lemonade? The outside warm air couldn't hold the moisture when it came in contact with the cold glass. The moisture is known as condensation.

In your home, the warm air is conducted through glass, walls, floors, and ceilings to the outdoors. When you weatherize your home you want to make sure that the warm air, as it cools, does not condense in your walls, on your windows or inside the insulation. One way to prevent condensation is by installing a vapor barrier towards the heated space. The vapor barrier prevents the moisture from leaving the heated space. We will keep reminding you about vapor barriers.

As with all systems, the key to success is understanding the way all the little things we do around the house can add up to the big picture. The good news is that we *can* make a difference. If you take even a fraction of the hints and tips in this book and apply them to your own home, you will see an immediate cost saving in your utility bills. Perhaps of even more importance, you will be helping to conserve the world's energy resources.

CHAPTER 1

—— GETTING READY —— FOR WINTER

So you're standing out in front of the house taking a good look at it. Nice house. Some warm memories inside. Pleasant place. Like it.

Just looking at it that way you couldn't tell, but maybe in addition to being a haven from the troubles of the world, it leaks like a busted balloon.

If that's the case, your home is the enemy of your budget, the destroyer of your plans to save for a vacation, and a secret ally of your predatory fuel supplier. Action is called for.

What you'll be striving for in your residential castle is a place that is secure against invaders. Today, though, the invaders threatening to steal your fortune are sneaky drafts, whistling winds, and the silent cold that comes in the dark of the night.

Your defenses are some tools and a few skills to tighten up the place against the invaders.

If you have some problems, you are aware of them when you are indoors, but the place to begin action to solve them is outdoors. There are various ways to deal with chilly drafts after they get in the house, but the better way is to stop them at the threshold, so to speak, before they get inside.

The effect you're reaching for is a more airtight package. In most older homes you don't need to worry about getting too airtight. The average place will continue to "breathe," and there will be plenty of fresh air, even after you do your best to fill the cracks.

And filling the cracks is essentially what you're up to. Here's why. A crack just ½-inch wide around an average door is just the same as a hole in your wall about four by six inches, or something like a missing window pane.

You will need a few tools for your security effort, but none of them are big, expensive items, and all of them are easy to use. As much time as you have available is what you need. You may not get the whole job done right away, but you can know that every part of your effort pays off in lower fuel bills and more comfortable living.

The best time to get at it is late summer and early fall. There's a morning nip in the air to give you an incentive, but it's still warm enough for easy working outdoors. Later on, when winter really hits, some of the things you'd like to do are difficult or impossible, because caulking and glazing compounds get balky in the cold, and patching cement won't set properly if the temperature is below freezing.

As you read this, is it already too late? Not necessarily. If it's the middle of December there are things you can still do this season, as well as good resolutions you can make about next year.

Here we go.

INSULATING AROUND WINDOWS AND DOORS

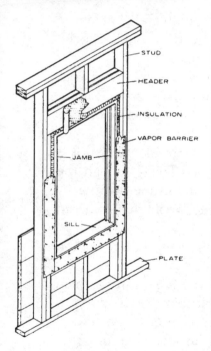

STUD

HEADER

INSULATION

VAPOR BARRIER

JAMB

SILL

PLATE

In new construction, a common place to find uninsulated is around window and door-frames. Small sections of insulation may be tucked in, but not packed so tightly that the insulating value is lost. The vapor barrier should face the heated room.

CAN COLD AIR GET IN DOORS?

A good place to start the security check is with the outside doors. They're in use many times a day all yearround, and are likely to lose their tightness of fit more rapidly than windows. Even if you have storm doors, the main doors need to be checked.

If you can see daylight around the door when it's closed, you have a major job on your hands. You may need to reset the hinges to get a better fit. However, adding lath strips on the inside of the door frame may do the job of covering those gaps, and then you can add weatherstripping to complete the job. If you feel cold air coming through, weatherstripping may be all that you need to tighten it up.

The full weather-stripping job on an outside door should cost about ten to fifteen dollars, and with a little annual adjusting, should last about five years. You may even save that amount in this winter's fuel costs, which means the job is paid for in the first year and clear profit for four years thereafter. That's a better return than putting your money in the bank.

There are several kinds of weatherstripping available. Some are better than others. Plastic adhesive V-strips are easy to install and will last a long time, depending on how much use the door gets. When installing the adhesive-backed weatherstripping, make sure to reinforce the adhesive with small tacks spaced approximately every six inches. Wood or aluminum door kits with vinyl bulb

TOO DRY?

Is you home too dry in the winter? Two signs of a house lacking moisture are:

1. Wooden furniture comes apart.

2. Those in the house complain of dry noses, and often have head colds.

weatherstripping last longer and are slightly more expensive.

The bottom of the door is the most important place to get a good seal, and the most difficult. If your threshold is quite worn, a tight weather-strip job is just about impossible, and a new threshold is called for. A soft wood such as pine planking is easiest to work with, but won't last a year in a heavy traffic spot. Make it a hard wood like oak, or get a metal doorsill.

To make a weathertight seal, you should install a door sweep on the bottom of the door. Several different products are available. Most are aluminum with a vinyl sweep made to withstand light, medium, or heavy use. Automatic door sweeps cause the sweep to lift as it comes over the inside carpet.

Almost as important as the door itself is the line where the doorframe meets the house. The door is probably slammed shut more than a thousand times a year, and that can loosen the caulking around the frame. You can buy a caulking gun and some tubes of caulking compound at any hardware store. Do it. Look for a siliconized acrylic latex caulk. Many caulks now come in various colors or are paintable. In addition to the bead of caulk around the doorframe, you'll be using the gun in a lot of other places, so it's a good investment.

You have a storm door? Good! Be sure the framing of the storm door is screwed tightly to the doorframe.

If you're installing a storm door, put down a bead of caulk across the top and down both sides before you install the frame. Then with the frame screwed in place, you're sure to have a tight and permanent seal against the breezes.

Do a good job on the front door, storm door and all, and you'll save $50 a year or more on your fuel bills, which makes it well worth the effort. You'll feel a lot more comfortable too!

WINDOWS MAY WASTE HEAT

Let's check the windows. That may sound like a big chore, if you have a lot of windows in your house. Here's a priority system: the west-facing windows are most likely to catch the prevailing winds, so do them first; the north-facing windows will be exposed to the coldest air, so do them second. The south-facing windows are probably the least vulnerable, so they can wait till last.

➡ Can you hear your windows rattle in a heavy windstorm? Yes? Then you have an important weather-stripping job to do. Did little breezes sometimes move the curtains even when the windows were closed last winter? Yes? Then you have both weatherstripping and caulking to complete.

WINDOWS SHUT — MONEY SAVED

The remodeled schoolhouse where I live still has four big windows (four feet wide by eight feet high). I like them, but they were an expense every winter. A year or two after I moved in I realized that there was plenty of summer ventilation from other sources, and the big windows were never opened. Now they are nailed shut, their cracks are caulked, and we save money every winter.

➡ Do you have some windows that are just for looking, but that you never open? Consider shutting them with a permanent seal. Close them securely, then caulk around all four sides. Add a single-pane (cheaper) storm window and bed in a bead of caulk when you install. The end result will be like the double-pane fixed window you may call a picture window in your living room.

➡ Cracked panes in your windows, or missing putty around the glass, will let cold air leak through. Get replacement panes for cracked or broken panes and tighten up.

➡ Don't use putty. Use plastic glazing compound. It's different. Putty dries out, cracks, and falls away. That's why you have the repair to make. A good glazing

TRICKS FOR USING GLAZING COMPOUND

Replacing a broken window in the winter is a bum chore, because the glazing compound gets stiff and intractable. If I have that chore ahead of me I tackle it with two cans of glazing compound; one in hand, and one keeping warmer indoors on the windowsill. By trading them back and forth, the job is possible. If you have only one can of glazing compound, tuck it under your jacket next to your warm body to keep it workable.

compound will last uncracked for at least ten years, and costs little more than ordinary putty. It's worth the difference.

Take a glob of glazing compound and roll it between your hands until it has the form of a piece of rope, or a snake. Then line it into the wedge made by the glass and the window frame. This makes a better seal than trying to press the compound in a dab at a time. For larger jobs, buy glazing compound in tubes which can fit into your caulking gun.

➡ When installing a window pane, there are several kinds

of glazier's tips or points you can use to hold the glass in place before you bead in the glazing compound. Particularly if you're up on a shaky ladder, the odds are good on your breaking the pane with your hammer when putting in some kinds of glazier's tips. Look for the kind with a nib sticking out. You can catch that nib with a screwdriver, tap the screwdriver handle with your hammer, and improve your odds considerably.

➡ Getting the glass replaced and reset is the right first step. That completed, a window that is still rattling needs weatherstripping. The most satisfactory method is to install V-strip or extruded plastic strips already shaped in a V. If you are planning on weatherstripping many windows, you will save money if your purchase the V-strip in 180-foot rolls. Here's an installation tip: make sure the window channels are free of dirt and grease. Clean with a damp rag before installing the V-strip. And, as with doors, reinforce the V-strip with small tacks.

➡ Another possible leakage area is around the window frame. A bead of caulking compound down both sides and at top and bottom should seal out the vagrant breezes, if the window itself is tight.

➡ Have you seen those clamshell locks on many double-hung windows? Their prime purpose isn't security, but to pull the sashes together to keep cold air from entering.

More on Infiltration — Air Sealing

Sealing the cracks and holes around windows and doors definitely reduces drafts and keeps you more comfortable. But did you know that there are many other significant ways that infiltration is taking place? Twenty to forty percent of your heating bill may be due to cold air entering your home or warm air leaving. The technical terms are *infiltration* and *exfiltration*.

What causes infiltration? The wind blowing against one side of your house is one way cold air gets in and warm air is pushed out. Another way is through the "chimney effect" or "stack effect". Without going into too much technical detail, heated air tends to rise. This creates a difference in pressure between the top and bottom of the house. At the top, air is pushed out Iexfiltration). Air is then sucked in from the bottom. In addition, combustion appliances — from boilers and furnaces to ranges and water heaters — contribute to air infiltration. As air is used during combustion it must be replaced by fresh air. Usually this fresh air is sucked into the house by whatever passageways are available.

All of the holes which were drilled for your plumbing stacks or electrical wires become pathways for warm air to leave your home. In the attic, the partition walls become an escape route for heated air. Sometimes there is nothing behind your kitchen or other built-in cabinets to stop your heat from going into the walls and up to the attic. These paths for cold air to get into your house and warm air to get out of your house are called *bypasses*.

Finding and sealing these major bypasses will definitely result in savings on your fuel bill. Now, there are specialists, often called "house doctors" or "air-sealing technicians" who are trained to find and seal these bypasses. One of their main tools is a "blower door". A blower door is basically a fan which is placed inside a doorway and attached to several instruments. Its purpose is to calculate how fast air is leaving your home. With this information, the air-sealing technican can make sure that your home is not sealed too tight. You will also know just how much was accomplished through the air-sealing by comparing the before and after blower door test.

Will air-sealing make your house too tight? Will it increase the possibility of radon entering your home? No. By using the blower door, you can make sure your house will not be sealed too tight. In addition, attention to sealing bypasses in the attic and basement reduces the chimney effect, one of the major driving forces which pulls any radon from the ground into your basement.

More and more weatherization professionals are learning about air-sealing and using blower doors. Air sealing techniques are also used extensively in new home construction.

WHAT ELSE CAN I DO?

Storm windows are an excellent buy, particularly in the northern climates. Wooden frames are more efficient than metal frames because they conduct less heat from inside to outside. Fixed storm windows are less expensive than storm and screen combinations (tripletrack) storm windows. The screens allow for ventilation without bugs in the summer.

Many storm window are now tested for their energy performance. A high quality storm will have an infiltration rate of less than .5 (one-half) cubic feet per minute with a fifteen miles-per-hour wind. Ask to see the manufacturer's literature on the product your are installing. Whatever kind you buy, make sure it is installed well and fits snugly.

➡ In aluminum storm windows, the heavier the gauge of the metal and the deeper the tracks, or grooves, that the windows slide in, the better job they will do for you. Make sure they are weather-stripped. Felt pile weatherstripping is most common for storms. Because metal is such a good conductor, look for a storm window with a "thermal break" to cut that flow of warm air out the metal edge of your storm window.

➡ When installing prefabricated aluminum tripletrack windows, put a bead of caulking compound between the frame of the house window and the new aluminum framing, to be sure there is a full seal to keep out drafts.

Then screw in place.

➡ If full storm windows aren't in your budget this year, consider plastic storm kits. Several inexpensive types of storm window kits are available. Reusable plastic

OLD STORM WINDOWS

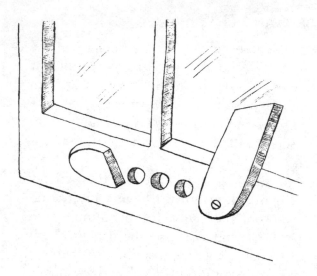

I remember storm windows from my youth: big, cumbersome items that were stored in the attic or the garage, if you bothered to take them down at all. A number was placed on each window frame and windowsill so that they could be matched when it was time to put up the windows. One-inch holes were drilled in the bottom of the frame and covered with a hinged flap that could be opened to let in a little fresh air. All told, a very efficient design. If you still have them, treasure them.

interior storm kits contain very clear plastic with narrow plastic strips to hold the window in place and adhere it to the window frame. These can last up to five years or more. Another easy-to-use storm window kit is installed with a hair dryer and usually lasts one season. Finally, six-mil polyethylene is sold in sheets and rolls at many hardware stores, and it will do a big job.

➡ With polyethylene sheeting, indoor installation is easier and performs better, but is less attractive than installing it on the outside. Indoors, you can put up the sheeting with masking tape, and it will cut back the breezes wonderfully.

➡ For outdoor installation, measure your plastic to the outer edges of the window frame, cut, then tack through ¼-inch wood slats to hold the plastic firmly to the window frame. A trim, neat job offers minimum opportunity for the wind to catch an edge and tear off the whole thing.

➡ For a house with smooth wooden siding, measure the plastic to extend beyond the window frame on all four sides and tack through the slats right into the siding.

CHECKING THE FOUNDATION

You may have to bend over often to make this final check of the exterior of your home.

Masonry work should be pointed before winter, which means filling the cracks in concrete foundations and facing brickwork. Your hardware store will have ready-mix mortar for the job, and they'll be glad to sell you a small trowel for applying.

Mix your patching and pointing mortar in an old bucket. Cleaning it out after you're finished will be darned near impossible. If you don't finish your job in one day, hose out whatever mortar remains in it; it won't keep overnight. When the job is finished you can swish the bucket out and hang it in the garage, if you have a place for that kind of storage.

The plank on top of your foundation wall is called a "sill plate." If there is a crack between it and the foundation, put the caulking gun to it and fill that crack. For any crack a half-inch or more wide, an expandable foam will work best. Look for an "ozone-friendly" foam, one which doesn't contain chlorofluorocarbons, more commonly referred to as cfcs.

If you have a major break in the foundation, patching may not be enough. Make a wooden frame, or form, that will cover the crack at least two inches on each side and at least an inch thick, then pour mortar into the form for a thorough job. Let it set at least twenty-four hours before removing the form.

HOW WE USE ENERGY

Pennsylvania State University says this is how energy is used at home:

Heating of space 57.5%
Water heating 14.9%
Refrigerating 6.0%
Cooking 5.5%
Air conditioning 3.7%
Lighting 3.5%
Television 3.0%
Food freezer 1.9%
Clothes drying 1.7%
Others 2.3%

It can be seen that the big energy users in the home are heating of space and water heating, totaling 72.4 percent. This is where the most can be accomplished in saving energy.

The lapped siding used in many traditional homes can develop cracks over the years, and the siding should be sealed with caulking. The best time to do it is just before painting. However, the caulking job doesn't have to make your house look like a patchy mess, because caulk comes paintable or in a variety of colors so that you can pick out a fairly close match. You should make sure that the walls have been insulated before you begin so that the siding won't have to be removed after you have taken the time to seal it.

Be sure that your cellar windows are closed tightly through the winter. Consider boarding over those cellar windows for the cold season, or at least given them a double polyethylene covering.

Evergreen shrubbery around the base of your home has much more than a decorative purpose: it cuts the force of the wind at your home's most vulnerable point. Those evergreens are most important on the northern and western sides, where the winds will be strongest.

Been thinking about a tool shed? There are metal structures you can put up in your yard, but you'll get more for your money with a shed built right against the house. There it will serve as dead-air insulation against the wall, and also stop the drafts from sneaking through that section of the foundation area.

If you're going to build an attached tool shed, the best location is on a west wall; next best is on a north wall, for fuel-saving purposes.

The same logic that applies to a tool shed applies to a dog house. A separate structure may be desirable, but one attached to the house has fuel-saving advantages.

If you have an outside tank for fuel oil, consider a framed cover for it. Sheltering it from the elements will minimize evaporation from sun heat, will tend to keep it from getting too cold for the oil to flow in subzero temperatures, will add some insulation and draft-cutting factors to your house, and will be more attractive.

About that cover for the oil tank: most local building codes wisely won't let you make a conventional airtight structure. Be sure it is well vented so fumes won't accumulate and potentially explode.

If you have perennial flower beds at the base of your house, you may bank them with bales of hay or straw in the fall to protect the plants. Good idea. While you're at it, take into account that the straw is extra insulation around the base of your house. Let your straw bed be deep and generous, but be sure to remove it in the spring or you'll run the risk of rotting the wood.

The next time you paint your house, or put on a new roof, keep in mind that the darker colors absorb heat from the sun, while those light, bright colors reflect heat away that you might be using to advantage.

CHAPTER 2
— SIMPLE STEPS FOR — EFFICIENT INSULATION

The purpose of insulation can be stated simply: to keep the heat where you want it.

HOW DOES INSULATION WORK?

Most insulating materials create "dead-air spaces." Since heated air wants to move quickly, these dead-air spaces slow down that air and it takes longer for the warm air to mingle with the colder air outside the heated space.

What you're after is to keep the coldest air from getting in your house at the bottom, and to stop the warm air from getting out through the walls or the top. In new home construction, full insulation of walls, attic, or roof is easy. In your existing home, insulating may be more difficult, but you probably can reach some of the important places.

It's important to keep the dead-air idea in mind. It's like the fishnet long johns that are worn by arctic explorers, or down jackets worn in northern climates. They will keep the body warmer than layers of solid clothing.

Good heat conductors are poor insulators. For example, a stone outer wall is poor in insulation value. The same can be said for brick and concrete. Sheet metal (for the so-called tin roof), single-pane glass, stucco, and roofing shingles all fall into the same category: very little insulation value.

Lumber, composition board, and earth walls have some insulation value, but the real winners are the expanded glass and mineral fibers you can buy as fiberglass, newspaper products like cellulose, or rigid foam boards.

Crumpled paper and dry straw also can serve that air-trapping purpose, but are a fire hazard and should never be used. Dry paper can catch fire even though it is encased in a tightly sealed box made of steel a quarter-inch thick.

A thorough job of insulating your attic, walls, and floor can save up to 50 percent on the winter fuel bills, so we're talking about the major item in this business of saving energy. The cheerful thing about this undertaking is that every step is profit. Even if you don't accomplish everything, each insulation area checked off on your list will be a money saver.

WHEN INSULATING, START AT THE TOP

The attic is one of the best places for saving money if your insulation is skimpy or nonexistent.

Let's say your attic is a completely unusable space under a truss roof and isn't insulated. You have two alternatives: blankets of fiberglass or bags of loose fill. If possible, select the loose fill so that the rafters can be completely covered. In this way, you will minimize the bypass created by the wood rafters. However, if the space is easy to get at, and the spacing of the rafters is a standard sixteen or twenty-four inches, fiberglass batts are a definite option. Again, the insulation will be more effective if you overlap the rafters.

If what's up is a crawling job with a lot of irregular spaces, choose the bags of loose material. You may be able to rent an insulation blower. This machine will enable you to pack more insulation into each cavity. The most common loose fill is cellulose, which is made from recycled newspapers and contains boron as a fire retardant.

Many attic insulation jobs can easily be do-it-yourself tasks. However, if you are also planning to insulate your walls with blown cellulose, you will probably need to hire a contractor.

HOW MUCH INSULATION DO YOU NEED?

It depends on the severity of your winters, how you heat your home and how much you can get into the area you want to insulate. You will probably want at least R-30, which is equivalent to about ten inches of insulation, in your attic.

WHAT ELSE DO YOU NEED TO KNOW BEFORE YOU INSULATE?

Don't forget about the vapor barrier. Standard insulation rolls and batts have a vapor barrier on one side. The vapor barrier should face the heated living space. With loose fill, put down six-mil polyethylene before installing the insulation, unless the spaces are so irregular or inaccessible that such a vapor barrier placement is impossible.

Be sure to place insulation out far enough to cover the top of the outer wall. At the same time, be sure you don't block the vents under the eaves, if there are any. That may mean putting a piece of scrap wood or cardboard at each end of each run with the loose fill to avoid plugging necessary ventilation.

In all likelihood you'll be running into light fixtures and a maze of wires up there. Unless the fixture is labeled "IC," be sure that it isn't accidentally covered during installation. Put baffles around the light fixtures and check for a minimum three-inch clearance. Insulation should never be in contact with bare wires. BARE WIRES! Call the electrician!

The loose fill is fire-resistant and can be in contact with the boxes that hold electrical connections. With batts and blankets, be sure that any paper coverings are peeled back or cut off to at least three inches away from any electrical junctions or fixtures.

Let's say now that you have an unfinished attic, but the floor is already in place. If you're not going to use the attic, and there's no reason at all to heat it, now or in the future, your best bet will be to put insulation between the ceiling and attic floor. If you want to do it yourself, you will need to take up the floor and put insulation between the exposed floor joists. Then you can put the floor back down again so the attic can be used as unheated storage space. Alternatively, you can get a contractor to install the insulation. The contractor will need to remove several boards, but will then be able to blow the insulation the length of the joists.

Alternatively, let's suppose the attic space is going to be used as a sewing room, play room, workshop, or other purpose that requires heating. Then you'll want to insulate the roof.

Chances are your roof beams are on 24-inch centers, so there will be standard batts in the six-inch fiberglass or rock wool insulation that will fit for insulating the roof. If yours is an older house you may not have those standard spacings, in which case you'll have to cut batts to fit, or buy sheets of polystyrene foam board and cut to fit. If you use the polystyrene foam board, the way to buy is by "R" numbers. In general, these panels have high insulation value for their thickness. Again, try to insulate to R-30 or more if possible.

Caution. These foam board panels release deadly toxic fumes if there is a fire in your home. They should be covered with Sheetrock to minimize that danger and meet most fire codes.

Some added notes on attics:

➡ When you're working up there, be sure you have boards to walk on and an extension light to help you see what you're doing. When walking on the floor joists, it only takes one slip to send you to the hospital, because that ceiling under you won't support you, and you'll fall right through.

➡ Overhead, be careful at all times to steer clear of the roofing nails that are sticking through, or you'll get that hole in your head you've been hearing about all these years.

➡ The end walls can also be hazardous, because the nails that secure the outer siding are almost certainly sticking through. If your house has any years on it at all, those roofing and siding nails are dirty and rusty, and good candidates to give you a serious infection. If you do get a puncture wound up there in the attic, don't mess around with it. Get to a doctor right away.

➡ Before you begin insulating, check the exposed roof areas for stains and discolorations on the wood. They indicate the presence of moisture. Be sure to find the source of moisture and assess its importance. For example, the moisture may be originate from a bathroom which vents to the attic. It may be due to a leaky roof. You could have a mess on your hands if you don't consider moisture as you weatherize your home. Wet insulation is ineffective, and may damage your home by holding moisture and causing rot.

WHAT ABOUT VENTILATION?

When you insulate your attic, you will want to make sure that any moisture which gets into your attic is whisked to the outdoors before it can condense in your insulation or on your roof. This is the purpose of ventilation. Usually a combination of high vents and low vents are best to insure that there is adequate air flow to move the moisture effectively. Vents can be installed in the gables, eaves, or roof.

We know it seems strange to intentionally allow cold air to come into your attic, but it's better than the damage which moisture can cause. If you have a vapor barrier in place, then you will need about half as much ventilation as when there is no vapor barrier. The rule of thumb is that for every 150 square feet of attic space without a vapor barrier, or 300 square feet with a vapor barrier, you will need approximately one square foot of ventilation.

Are you planning on converting your attic to living space? Perhaps the attic rooms you want to use will heat themselves in the winter with what naturally rises from the house beneath, unless the attic floor is well insulated. Running heating ducts to the attic may be unnecessary.

If you expand your living space by making use of attic rooms, avoid running water pipes up there if you can. If there are no water pipes, the rooms can be closed off when not in use, with no danger of pipes freezing and breaking.

If you have an unheated attic with flooring for storage ease, then there's a place for that worn carpeting when you re-do the living room. Put it down on the attic floor. It may not look wonderful, but who cares? It will add a measure of insulation, and you may be the first on your block with the luxury of wall-to-wall carpeting in the attic!

Check the door to your unheated attic, and to any other unheated area in the house. That door should be treated like a door to the outdoors: closed whenever possible, and weather-stripped if needed. You can also insulate the back of this door with vinyl-backed fiberglass wrap, the same material which may be insulating your hot water tank.

When you plan to open extra rooms in the attic, be sure to include the cost of Thermopane windows or storm windows in your estimates, or the project may wind up costing you a lot more than you imagined. The heat loss through attic windows can be greater because it is windier so high up.

WHAT ABOUT INSULATING THE WALLS?

If yours is an older home that has never been insulated, you should definitely find out whether the walls can be insulated. If you need insulation, the easiest method is for a contractor to blow cellulose into the walls from the outside. The contractor will remove enough of the siding to drill a hole through the wall or clapboard. Thenhe will insert a hose through which cellulose will be densely packed in the wall cavity.

If you are planning to remodel, the easiest way to insulate is to install fiberglass batts from the interior. You can remove the indoors side of the outer walls and start insulating. Your first layer will probably be wallpaper, then plaster, then wooden lath strips, then paper, then — I hate to tell you. Inside the walls will be the dust of the centuries, augmented by whatever the mice have left behind. Have handy a shovel, broom, and vacuum cleaner.

When you get into the wall you may discover that the vertical studs aren't spaced evenly, so standard insulation won't fit. You may also find braces between the studs. Those are firebreaks. They tend to slow down a fire that might otherwise run up through the walls unchecked.

When the outer wall is exposed, caulk all the gaps to the exterior. This will keep cold air from coming inside. Next, fit in the insulation as best you can, first filling in all the cracks around doors and windows. The vapor barrier should be on the warm side of the wall. If there isn't a vapor barrier on the insulation you are using, then a sheet cover of four-mil to six-mil polyethylene is indicated.

If yours is a newer home and not insulated the process of redoing the walls isn't going to be too difficult. You may even be able to salvage the panels of Sheetrock if you are very careful when taking them down.

A final thought.

When there is any amount of insulation material to install, there is one super-tool you'll do well to buy. It's the staple gun. There's really no easy way to install batts or blankets of insulation without a staple gun, especially if you're doing overhead work. It's also just about essential for handling polyethylene sheets. Keep it around the house when the insulating chores are completed. You'll find yourself using it for lots of chores, and indispensable if you get into reupholstering a favorite chair.

SAVING MONEY IN THE BASEMENT

It's sometimes a bit more complicated to figure out the best approach to saving money in the basement.

Do you have an unheated basement that is used only for storage and utilities? Then you should consider insulating the basement ceiling. In effect, this is insulating the floor of your first story. After you insulate, your first floor will feel warmer and more comfortable.

Right now the basement may be unintentionally heated from the heating system and pipes. When you insulate the ceiling and pipes, the basement will get somewhat colder. Be sure that this lower temperature will be acceptable when you have chores to do in the basement.

Batts or blankets of fiberglass are the easiest bet. Before you rush out to buy, measure. If the floor joists are spaced on 16-inch or 24-inch centers, you're in luck, because those are the standard widths for batts or rolls of insulation. The standard length for batts is six feet, so you can figure how many batts you're going to need for the under-floor area you're working with. The insulation should be installed flush to the ceiling to minimize air or moisture flow between the insulation and the ceiling.

As you've discovered by now, standard insulation rolls and batts have a vapor barrier on one side. Again, you want that vapor barrier to be facing the warmth, which means in an under-floor installation the vapor barrier goes up. However, it is really quite difficult to get an effective and continuous vapor barrier. An equally important consideration is keeping the fiberglass fibers covered. A building material called Tyvek can be used on the basement side of your insulation to cover the fiberglass insulation.

If you have a problem of fitting, it may be solved by

rolling out the insulation and then tacking up lengths of wire mesh or chicken wire.

Caution. That under-floor insulation, if you do your job right, may leave the cellar colder. That's okay, unless there are water pipes running through the cold area. The cold water pipes may need to be wrapped to prevent freezing, and the hot water pipes should be wrapped to avoid chilling the water you are paying to heat. If you have a boiler or forced-air furnace in that space you're making colder, you will definitely need to insulate the heating pipes or heating ducts leading from the furnace.

HEATING DUCTS:

Before insulating the heating ducts, check the seams between sections to be sure they are tight. If you have any doubts, use silver duct tape which is available in several widths for sealing those duct junctures before you install insulation. The wider tape is easier to work with. Duct insulation is available in two-inch thickness and is easy to install. Seal the joints between sections of insulation with high-temperature vinyl tape. Duct tape is also okay.

PIPE INSULATION:

High temperature closed-cell foam for hot water (hydronic) baseboard heating systems usually comes in sections six feet long. They are available for any heating system pipe diameters. For steam heating systems, various sizes of high temperature fiberglass sleeve insulation are available.

Caution. If you have steam pipes, check to see if they insulated with asbestos. If so, do not disturb this insulation without checking with your local health department to find out the regulations and procedures you must follow.

All you have underneath is a crawl space? Insulation will do a good job there, too. Choose a day when you are feeling calm and even-tempered, and wear old clothes.

An under-house crawl space will try your patience, skin your knuckles, and certainly leave you with bumps on your head and cobwebs in your ears.

In handling insulation such as fiberglass, a mask over your nose and mouth is a wise idea to avoid breathing those tiny glass particles.

Plan one trip into the crawl space just for measuring. Do a good job and make notes. Then you can cut your materials outside, instead of struggling with that part of the job while you're flat on your back with spiders crawling into your collar and dust sifting into your eyes.

Your materials are six-mil polyethylene for a vapor barrier, R-11 or R-19 blankets of fiberglass — that's the stuff that's about three or six inches thick respectively — and strips of scrap wood for nailing. The board to hold the batts in place can be scrap 1x2s or anything else that's handy. All you want is a weight to keep the insulation positioned where you need it.

How did you get into that crawl space? Through a trap door, an entry hatch, or a ventilation opening? Be sure any outer entry is closed tightly, weather-stripped and insulated, if possible, or some of your effort will have been in vain.

Another suggestion: Put a layer of polyethylene on the ground to keep moisture from getting into the insulation, especially with dirt floors.

Chances are there are some pipes leading to the kitchen sink going up an outside wall in the crawl space, and maybe some other water pipes as well. Before you leave, be sure they are well wrapped against the cold. They may not have frozen in other years, but now that under-floor area is going to be colder.

The security of those exposed water pipes is doubly important if the pipes are PVC (polyvinyl chloride) or another of the plastics. The plastic pipes aren't as likely to burst as copper or galvanized, but they are the devil to thaw if they are blocked with ice, because you can't use either blowtorch heat or electric resistance treatment on them.

Providing for summertime ventilation in the crawl space is important to avoid wood rot and mildew problems. Take that into account as you are installing your insulation.

On the other hand, let's say you have a cellar area that is used for a variety of purposes that require it to be heated, like laundry areas, play areas, and indoor gardening efforts. Then insulating the walls is the task at hand, and it's easy, even if the existing walls are poured concrete or cinder blocks. As usual, make sure you seal all the gaps first!

On the interior of your outside walls, you'll be building another facing wall with 2x4s. The bottom plate will just sit on the concrete floor, not nailed to anything. The top plate can be nailed to the floor joists above it, then the vertical studs should be cut to fit snugly, or slightly force-fit, to be sure the whole works is going to stay in place.

Insulation to fit on 24-inch centers, R-11 (about 3.5 inches thick), will do well, so your vertical studs must be positioned accordingly. This isn't a bearing wall holding up house weight, so your construction can be simple.

Install the insulation from the top down to where the frost line is expected to be. In the northern states, that may mean running the insulation all the way down to the floor. The vapor barrier on the insulation panels should be facing the room. If the batts or rolls you buy don't have a vapor barrier, sheets of six-mil polyethylene should be installed over the insulation after it is put in place. A continuous vapor barrier is most effective.

Cover the insulated wall with whatever suits your fancy, taking into account the fact that cellars can be damp. Sheetrock or gypsum board can be quickly ruined if there is water on the floor. So can plywood, unless it is exterior construction grade, which is expensive. Plain pine wood paneling is a good bet.

If floor water may be a problem, you can run almost any kind of wallboard down to about six inches from the floor, then cover the gap with a board molding of eight-inch planks. Don't run the wallboard down to the floor, or it will act like a wick and draw water up to ruin your wall.

Above your new wall, between the floor joists and at both ends, will be exposed areas where insulation is needed. Place it vertically to meet the floor above and also across the top of your new wall. This won't be the most beautiful thing that's happened to your house, but it is practical, and you won't see it at all when you finally get around to putting in a ceiling.

CHAPTER 3

—— KEEPING COMFY ——
ROOM BY ROOM

Some people think that conservation can be boiled down to this: "How miserable can you stand to be?" Well, that's one approach. It starts off with the plea to turn your thermostat down to 60°F. and smile nobly as you shiver. Fortunately, conservation does not have to result in discomfort. With a little awareness and effort, you can trim your energy use without great sacrifice. That's what this chapter is about.

One of the easiest ways to save fuel is through attentiveness to your thermostat setting. Your heating system and lifestyle will determine how much flexibility you have in setting your thermostat.

THERMOSTAT: THE KEY TO SAVINGS

Thermostats, where they are located in your home, and how you set them, can be instrumental in determining the size of your winter's fuel bill.

➡ When you'll be out for an evening, turn down the thermostats. If you'll be away for a weekend or more, lower the thermostats to 55°F., or to the lowest temperature setting before "off." You'll save on heating without chancing a freezeup of your water pipes.

➡ When you can shut your house for a few days or more, you'll save a little on the operation of the refrigerator and freezer, which won't need to work so hard to maintain their cool.

➡ How low can your home thermostats be set? We've gotten accustomed to 68°F. to 70°F. as a comfortable norm. Reduce the heat just one degree at a time and try it for a week. Each one-degree drop for twenty-four hours means about a three percent reduction in your fuel bill and — gradually — you might be able to go down three or even four degrees comfortably and save a chunk of money.

➡ Try turning down the thermostat five to ten degrees at night, and then turning it up again in the morning when the coffee is heating. If you can get used to that, you'll save five to ten percent of your heating bill.

One common myth is that by reducing the thermostat for only a few hours, it will take more heat to bring your home back up to the desired temperature. This really is not so. You will save money and fuel because your heating system will not have to keep your home so warm. You will use less energy overall even when you warm up your house from a cooler temperature.

➡ For greater ease and comfort, install a programmable setback thermostat. They are available for most gas and oil central heating systems. In this way, you can have your heating system come on before you get up in the morning and lower the heat just as you get into bed. You may not even notice that you are setting back your thermostat. Most of these thermostats come with two setbacks. Therefore, you can also set back the thermostat for the hours that people are in school and at work.

➡ Some setback thermostats are able to have different setbacks for weekends. If you frequently forget to setback your thermostat, the programmable set back thermostats will be a great investment. Even if you are already pretty good at remembering, these devices can frequently enable you to set back the thermostat a few extra degrees, providing you with additional savings.

➡ If you happen to heat with electricity, you can take advantage of the individual room thermostats which make it possible to shut off unused rooms, have cool settings in some rooms and warmer settings in others. Using this feature of electric heat will definitely minimize your fuel bills. If you have a thermostat that does control a relatively large area, you should still consider a setback thermostat. You will need an electrician for this installation.

The old-fashioned custom among the wealthy — a little fireplace in each bedroom — was an early variation on the zone-heating theme. One of the servants would go upstairs and light each fire a half-hour before bedtime to take off the chill. Later, as the fire died down and the room cooled, the occupant was asleep and wasn't made uncomfortable. Getting up in the morning could be a chiller unless the servant crew was instructed to kindle new fires before the folks woke up.

➡ Do you need to talk yourself into a lower thermostat setting? Here's an argument. Your plants are healthier in the cooler air.

➡ The health of your plants isn't in the same discussion with your personal comfort? All right, you'll be healthier in the cooler air. Your body will burn a few more calories keeping you warm, thereby helping you to lose the weight you wanted to lose anyway, to improve your general health. Besides, if you've already insulated and tightened your home, you will probably be just as comfortable at lower temperatures.

➡ When it's time to open the windows for a little fresh air indoors in the spring, remember to turn down the thermostats. Those cool breezes that feel so good will send your furnace on a fuel-burning rampage unless the thermostats are reset.

➡ Planning a good-sized party? Turn the thermostats down. Each guest is the equivalent of a 175-watt heater, and the gang will warm up the place without the furnace or the heating units in operation.

ECONOMICAL LIGHTING

Want to slow down that spinning electric meter? Be careful how you use lights in your home. Here are three ways.

1. Only use high-wattage reading lamps for reading or working. Candles or 25-watt bulbs offer plenty of light for evening conversation, create a pleasant mood for talking, and will reduce electric bills.

2. When you have a choice between incandescent light bulbs and fluorescent lights, choose the fluorescents. They use much less electricity for the same amount of light. You may still have bed memories about the ghastly blue tone the fluorescent tubes used to put out? Check your store for the newer, warm-tone screw-in light bulbs. They are much more flattering, and closer to a daylight radiance.

3. Dark walls and ceilings may be dramatic, but they absorb light. Pastels or white on walls and ceilings will give maximum illumination with fewer light fixtures burning in the evening, and will make a room with drapes open pleasantly light without electricity during daylight hours.

SPEAKING OF DRAPES

By closing drapreies and shades at night, you can cut your heat bill. Your existing draperies will be more effective in reducing heat loss if they are heavy or lined fabric.

Pull them back during the day, of course, for free light and heat. In fact, you'll do well to install your drapery rods well over the wall on each side of the windows to gain full light and heat benefit by pulling drapes all the way off the windows during daylight.

If you need draperies, consider insulating window shades. Typically, these are made of fabric with special insulating qualities. Another desirable feature is an edge seal to keep any drafts from coming through your windows. Do-it-yourself insulating shades are a less expensive option.

Are you on a low budget? It is a practical decorator touch to hang old patchwork quilts as window draperies. They'll be heavy enough to do a good job, easy to hang, and will certainly be interesting. Check your local thrift shop.

How to Save Heat — and Money

A new door here, new carpeting there, and a change in habits for all members of the family. These things can add up to big energy — and money — savings.

Read through this list, then check off the ones that would save you money.

- ❏ Don't leave the room without closing the closet door. There's no need to spend hard-earned money heating storage spaces. For a luxury touch, clothes you're going to wear can be taken out the night before into the room warmth. Be your own valet and save money.

- ❏ Take those beautiful Oriental throw rugs off the floor and hang them on the walls where people can see and enjoy them, and where they will serve as additional insulation.

- ❏ Carpeting on floors even in bathroom and kitchen is a heat-saver and comfort-maker. Durable carpeting is available that is quite practical for these locations. In the bathroom particularly, stepping out of the tub onto a cozy carpet is so much nicer than bracing your toes for these cold tiles. The practical advantage is that a bathroom thermostat can then be set much lower without any discomfort

- ❏ Is there a doorway between the first and second floors of your home, or on up into the attic? If not, you should have one. Stairwells act like chimney flues, conducting heat to the top of the house where you need it less. A door may be easy to construct and will tend to keep the heat downstairs where you need it.

❐ Time for school? Make a habit of getting all the kids out the door at once each day, instead of a separate opening and closing for each one. It may save enough for extra Christmas presents for all.

❐ Think about an outdoor doghouse. Remember, your pup's ancestors lived outdoors for centuries, and he can adapt to being outdoors all year-round, unless he happens to be one of the few tropical breeds like a Chihuahua. The wintertime advantage to you is no more opening and closing the door zumteen times a day to let him in and out — and resultant heat loss with each opening.

❐ Also with the dog outdoors, you may spend less time with the vacuum cleaner humming to pick up dog hairs.

❐ Make sure your thermostat is located on an interior wall, away from drafts. You don't want your thermostat to call for heat every time the door opens!

❐ Double doors at the principal entryway make a convenient foyer for winter boots, and also cut heat loss as people go in an out.

❐ Do you have a game room with a Ping-Pong table? Close it off with a well-fitting door and let it be cooler than the rest of the house. The action of the game will keep the players warm.

❐ Planning a home workshop? Since the room will not be used regularly, keep it off the main heating system and let it be cool between uses. Warm it with a separate heater or a small wood stove.

❐ Having the garage within your house framework is convenient in many ways, but be sure to have a separate door for going in and out to the yard or driveway. Every time you open the big garage door is like taking off the side of your house, and costs plenty in lost heat.

❏ Check around for those relatively useless appliances, and put them on the top shelf of the closet. Singly they don't use a lot of electricity, but together the electric toothbrush, electric shoe-shiner, electric car-washer and the like are items you don't really need.

❏ A rug in the children's play area gives warmth for playing on the floor than wood or tile. The new indoor-outdoor carpets made of synthetic yarns will take a lot of punishment and are quite stain-resistant.

❏ In redoing a bathroom a few years back I was stuck for a way to locate the warm air outlet. I finally placed it right over the tub/shower. I didn't know it, but that was a happy inspiration. The warm air blowing down is delightful either for tub bath or shower purposes.

❏ Go for soft, warm colors in the north rooms where direct sunlight is not available to cheer things up. You'll be surprised at the effect color has on how comfortable you feel.

❏ Don't forget to close those chimney dampers if you have a fireplace or stove not in use. An open chimney will exhaust more heat than an open window.

IN SUMMER IT'S THE HEAT AND THE HUMIDITY

There's lots you can do to keep cool in the summer. You'll be more comfortable this way, and if you have an air conditioner, you'll be saving energy as well.

In the summer, keep an eye peeled for extra lights burning, particularly incandescent bulbs. They furnish more heat than light and cause your air conditioner to work harder.

An air conditioner's filter should be cleaned or replaced at least once a month. This reduces the load on the unit, thereby decreasing operating costs.

An air conditioner operates most efficiently when placed on the shady side of your house — generally the north side.

Set your air conditioner thermostat no lower than 78°F., and shut it off if there's a breeze blowing that would cool things off through open windows.

Compare products before you buy an air conditioner. Look for the Seasonal Energy Efficiency Rating (SEER) that you'll find on most appliances today. The higher the number, the more cooling it will produce for a given amount of electricity.

With an air conditioning unit, bigger isn't necessarily better. A unit bigger than you need for the space to be cooled will make the air clammy and uncomfortable; while a unit too small will just work away burning kilowatt hours and still not cool you.

In regard to humidity, in summer you're looking for just the opposite effect from winter: low humidity. The kitchen and laundry areas are moisture-makers, so keep them closed off from the rest of the house as much as possible.

Humidity again: When you take a shower, open the bathroom window to let the moisture out.

More on humidity: In the summer, be sure to cover the pots on the stove when you're cooking to minimize the steam escaping into the room.

The covered pot, incidentally, is a good idea any time. It holds the heat in where it will do the cooking, rather than letting it escape into the room. The covered pot will come to a boil faster, saving fuel when you're making coffee, boiling eggs, or doing any other cooking business that calls for a boil.

Since warm air rises, in the summer you'll do well to open upstairs and attic windows to let the heat escape.

Then, in the cool of the evening let the more temperate air into the house and close the windows first thing in the morning to keep that cool air inside.

Awnings can really be a help in the summer. Particularly on the south windows, awnings will keep the sun away while still letting the light and breezes through. A heavy duck cloth, or plastic panels, either one in a light color or white, will be most effective.

A large window fan costs one-fifth as much as an air conditioner, and uses only one-forth as much power. Perhaps the most effective place to put it is in an attic window where it will push the hot air out of the house and draw the cooler air in through the downstairs windows. Bright pastel colors and crisp, cheery plants indoors and out will help to make your home feel cooler.

For cooling breezes in the spring and fall, open windows from the top to exhaust excess heat without making drafts that might trigger the thermostat.

You'll be cooler in a minimum amount of loosely-fitting clothing, but some clothes will help you feel cooler because the moisture evaporating from them as you perspire will feel good on your skin.

So, you make do with what you have, thinking all the time about what the next steps may be — which is the subject of another chapter.

FIVE EASY WAYS TO CUT HEATING COSTS

1. For many people, home heating bills can be cut ten percent or more with one simple move: have the furnace cleaned and adjusted properly. If yours is an oil burner, that means at least an annual inspection by a qualified technician.

2. While your oil burner is under discussion, find out if it is a "conventional" or a "retention head" burner. The latter is much more efficient. These use smaller fuel nozzles and save as much as fifteen percent on your fuel bill.

3. Forced warm-air furnaces need to have their air filters

cleaned or replaced at least twice each winter. A clogged filter chokes off the necessary breathing of the furnace and makes it work harder.

4. When you're rearranging furniture, be sure that radiators, warm-air registers or heating units aren't blocked from the proper functioning. If there's an arrangement you "must" have that blocks heat flow, let it wait until summer when it won't affect heating efficiency.

5. A little extra humidity permits a lower thermostat setting without discomfort. Some furnaces will accept a humidifying system easily and inexpensively. If that's not the case with you, try pans of water on radiators or heat registers to put a little moisture in the air.

CHAPTER 4

—— ECONOMY IN THE —— KITCHEN

In many aspects of our living, our daily functioning is made possible by habits we follow. If we had to think about how to brush our teeth, how to tie our shoes, how to put on a jacket — we wouldn't get started in the morning. We can do all those things almost without thinking, so they get done smoothly and quickly.

Those same habits can be ruinous when the monthly fuel bills arrive, because the inexpensive fuels of the past have led us into very wasteful practices, particularly in the kitchen. To achieve important economies doesn't necessarily mean drastic change in your style of living, but it certainly does mean programming yourself with a new set of habit patterns.

Some parts of our lives are optional, but not cooking and eating. What happens in the kitchen is absolutely necessary, and is going to happen every day. That's the reason why a careful examination of how fuel energy is used in the kitchen can be vital to your overall economy plan.

Another truth: Because using the kitchen is an everyday event for all the members of the household — and the kitchen may be the place where much of the shared life takes place — the development of new habits in the kitchen may raise the family consciousness about energy uses in general, and so spill over into other aspects of fuel saving.

Just one example may serve to illustrate. After a meal, we all know it is sensible to put leftover foods in the refrigerator. We all know if they are left out on the kitchen counter overnight, or even for several hours, they'll turn bad and need to be thrown away. There are two ways to use the refrigerator, though.

One way is to take the foods from the table and the pans from the stove and — probably in several trips — stack them in the refrigerator for later use. This way your refrigerator will be gasping for breath and laboring hard to keep its cool, what with hot foods, hot pans, and hot dishes to chill, and the door opening and closing several times.

Opening and closing the refrigerator door is costly. Cold air rushes out as soon as the door is opened. The more frequently the door is opened, the more cold air rushes out.

A better way is to put the leftovers in storage containers and let them sit on the counter for a half-hour or so until they cool a little. Then, all in one operation, they can be placed in the refrigerator for storage and later use.

There isn't much difference between those two methods. It's really no more than exchanging an old set of habits for a new set. Considering, though, that the process takes place in your kitchen several hundred times a year, if it saved you no more than a penny a meal (and it will save more than that) you're looking at a saving of $11 a year just in the way the refrigerator is used after mealtime. Eleven dollars here, seventy-five cents there, three dollars the other place; they all add up to make a significant difference, just by changing habits.

There are, of course, other avenues to saving that require investments of time and money. Make no mistake. They're worthwhile. It may be, though, that habit changes in the kitchen and elsewhere will save the most of all with the least effort.

Cool Cash Savings

There's money to be saved in your refrigerator. You may

be spending more than you need to just by running your refrigerator at a cooler setting than is required. Put an ordinary household thermometer in the refrigerator for a half-hour or so. If it registers colder than 40° F., change to a warmer setting and check it again.

While you're at it, check the door gaskets all the way around by closing the door on a dollar bill. If the bill slips out easily at any place, you're wasting money. You may be able to correct the problem by putting paper strips or thin cardboard behind the gasket where you spot the leak, or by adjusting the latch. If those don't do it, a new gasket is a good investment and isn't hard to install.

Here are some thoughts: When you stand with the refrigerator door open, thinking about what you'd like to have, you're running up the cost of that snack. Do your best to imagine what's inside before you open the door, and then go directly to it. Try to teach your children this habit, too.

Help yourself and your family by putting a checklist on the refrigerator door, rostering what's inside and also crossing off what's been eaten. That's the snack menu, and it can save many a door opening.

Get organized before meals so that everything needed can be taken out and placed at the ready on the kitchen counter with just one opening of the refrigerator door. Don't forget the catsup.

After coming home from the store, empty all the shopping bags on the counter, put all the items that need refrigeration in one place, *then* open the refrigerator door.

After dinner, think about storing the leftovers in the way outlined at the beginning of this chapter, with particular attention to the business of covered containers. This is particularly important with frost-free models, where moisture is drawn from the foods to condense on the refrigerating coils causing the defrost cycle to operate more often. If you don't have covered refrigerator containers, put the leftovers in cereal bowls and cover with a plate.

Convenient plastic containers can be bought in many stores, but you can also recycle peanut butter jars, cottage cheese containers, and similar packages with lids that can be cleaned to use for storage.

That frost-free feature certainly is a convenience, but a standard refrigerator that must be defrosted by hand a few times a year will use less electricity. Also remember when you're buying your next refrigerator that if you really do want the frost-free convenience, look for a model with a power saver switch. It turns off the defrost heater when humidity is low in the winter and may cut operating costs by as much as sixteen percent.

While you're refrigerator shopping, look at the yellow Energy Guide and ask for the manufacturer's information on average annual operating costs. These may vary by as much as $100 a year for the same size model.

When the kids grow up and have nests of their own, that big refrigerator you once needed may become a liability. A refrigerator operates most efficiently when it's full, and chances are you don't use its capacity. Consider giving one of the kids the big box and buying a smaller model.

When choosing where your refrigerator is placed, keep it away from heat-producers like ovens and dishwashers. An outside wall is a fair idea, particularly if it's a north wall that will tend to be cool both summer and winter.

And be sure there is adequate air space around the refrigerator, to let the motor heat escape readily. If it's been running hot, you could save as much as three to four dollars a month.

FREEZERS CAN BE EXPENSIVE

Most refrigerators today have a freezer compartment. You

may also have a separate freezer, or be thinking about one. Here are some freezer economies.

- For openers, a freezer will likely be one of your most expensive electrical appliances to operate. A manual-defrost, 14-cubic-foot model will use about 100 kilowatt hours of electricity each month. Multiply your kwh rate (if it isn't shown on your utility bill, call the power company) by that usage to find your cost.

- You'll use 50 percent more electricity with an automatic defrost model. Weigh that against the modest effort of defrosting once a month.

- Consider your separate freezer as if it were a supermarket annex. Plan your meals for several days — even a week — and transfer the freezer foods to the freezer compartment of the refrigerator all in one "shopping trip."

- Keep items for which there is a frequent call, like ice cream and orange juice, in the freezer compartment of the refrigerator so the big freezer won't need to be opened so often.

- Transfer big items like hams, roasts, and turkeys from the freezer or frozen food compartment to the refrigerator a day in advance. That way they will thaw gradually and help to cool the refrigerator while they're doing it.

- Recommended temperature for frozen foods is 10° F. Put a household thermometer in your freezer and check the temperature. If it's colder than necessary, change the control setting and check again. You may want to run the temperature setting down to zero when you are putting away the harvest from your garden or adding many things at once to be frozen. Don't forget to reset it.

- Keep your freezer as full as possible. The bulk of the foods will retain the cold better than empty air, making for more economical operation.

➡ Position your separate freezer in a cool part of the cellar, on the back porch, or out in the garage. These are cooler places, particularly during the winter, and your freezer motor won't need to work so hard. Be sure to check your instructions to make sure your model can withstand freezing temperatures without damage.

➡ You'll get extra mileage from your freezer — and your oven — when you cook oversize batches of favorite casseroles and freeze the extra in meal-size packages.

➡ If you have an orderly mind, you can plan to have your separate freezer empty during the growing season when you're eating fresh foods from the garden. Then you can shut it off during the warmest months when it works the hardest.

➡ Putting your frozen foods in well-marked containers and keeping the frozen supplies in easily recognized categories, will make everything easier to find, and therefore mean less time that the door is open while you are searching for something.

➡ A freezer inventory is a good idea. It can be a sheet or small notebook on the wall or on a shelf near the appliance. Menu planning can be done from the inventory, which could even include a locator chart so each item can be found easily. Again, less time with the door open.

➡ Baking a pie? Bake three or four, and cool and freeze the extras. You'll save money on your oven usage, and those frozen pies will come out weeks or months later ready for a quick warm-up before going to the table.

➡ Leftover waffle batter? Make the waffles, put them in a plastic bag and freeze them. They'll perk up almost like newly made with a few minutes in the toaster or in your tabletop broiler-oven.

➡ A last - but not least - thought on freezers: The upright models may be somewhat more convenient to use, but every time you open the door the cold "falls out." Chest-type freezers are much more frugal in operation.

COOKING THE ORIENTAL WAY

In China, cooking fuel has been a scarce and expensive commodity for centuries. To meet the need, the Chinese have developed a method called stir-frying. They do it in a utensil called a wok. You can buy one if you want to be thoroughly authentic, or you can use your frying pan. The meat and vegetables are cut or sliced into small bite sizes and cooked in a moment in hot oil. A full meal cooks in minutes. Tasty, economical, and more nutritious, too.

Cooking fuel is also precious in overcrowded Japan, where tempura cooking has become one of the answers. Again, it is bite-size pieces in hot oil, but they are dipped in a tasty batter first, quickly fried, and then dunked in one of several appetizing sauces. Another economical treat.

A more conventional way to use the same principle is to cut vegetables into bite-size pieces and cook them in a steamer. They'll cook nearly as fast as with the boiling water treatment, and retain more taste and nutrition in the process.

Try to cut back on the number of burners you fire up to prepare a meal. The ideal here is something like the pot roast where a complete meal is cooked on one burner. There are many variations, including that all-time favorite, corned beef and cabbage with boiled potatoes.

When boiling water, as for soft-boiled eggs or macaroni, turn the burner down as far as you can and still maintain the boil. The water is going to get just so hot and no hotter. Too much heat only makes steam — and wastes money.

When boiling anything on the stove, use the least amount of water possible. The cooking will be done more quickly, you'll waste fewer of the nutrients, and, by keeping the lid on, you will minimize the danger of "boiling dry".

Don't Forget the Oven

Whether it's gas or electric, the oven in a conventional stove is an energy glutton. The problem is compounded if the oven has a preheating feature, and gets even worse if it's the self-cleaning variety. Let's take a look.

One answer to oven efficiency is to get maximum use when you fire it up. For instance, if you plan to bake pies, time it so you can cook an oven dinner in the same cycle.

Having roast beef or pork? Try baked acorn squash for the vegetable, and put some baked potatoes on the side. That way the whole meal can be oven-baked in one shot, instead of firing up the stove burners, too.

Do you like mashed potatoes with your roast beef? My mother baked the potatoes; when they were done, she scooped them from their skins and mashed them. After mashing, they went back into the skins with a pat of butter and a little paprika on top, and back into the oven. Superb.

Casseroles are limited in their variety only by the extent of your imagination. Any time you are baking cakes, pies, cookies, or even a roast, plan to bake a casserole at the same time. Start with cookbook recipes, and then get inventive on your own.

After baking in the winter, leave the oven door open until the oven is cool. No sense wasting that heat. Conversely, in the summer try to schedule some of the baking for the cool of the evening, with obvious advantages.

Before putting frozen foods in the oven, thaw them in the refrigerator or on the kitchen counter. They'll cook more quickly, therefore at less expense.

For desserts and snacks, consider goodies like sliced fresh peaches with milk and sugar, dried fruits, salted nuts, and the instant puddings that don't require cooking. Over the course of the year they'll be much more economical than pies and cakes that need to be baked.

A small countertop broiler-oven can often be used for

single casseroles or individual meals, and use less electricity. With that appliance, plus the oven and broiler in your stove, you'll have three choices. Use the smallest that will do the job.

Don't forget to use your slow cooker. It uses much less energy than an oven or stove.

A microwave is even better in that it consumes very little energy. Take advantage of your microwave for at least some part of every meal—you'll see a savings on your utility bill!

HEAT IN THE KITCHEN

The heating units in electric appliances continue to radiate after being turned off. With a little practice you can learn to turn off the heat a few minutes early and finish with the leftover heat.

A pressure cooker uses much less fuel than a conventional pan. When preparing boiled potatoes, for instance, a pressure cooker will use 30 percent less energy, doing the job in half the time.

Quick cup of coffee? Your electric coffee pot will boil water more quickly at less cost than a pan on the stove.

The kitchen exhaust fan keeps the house cleaner, but in the winter it is also pushing precious warm air into the outdoors. Some of the need for the exhaust fan results from the steam and grease spatters caused by cooking at higher temperatures than needed. An awareness of this situation can lead to twofold savings.

SHOULD YOU RETIRE YOUR SMALL APPLIANCES?

Your electric carving knife, electric can opener, mixer, orange juice maker, sealer for plastic bags, sandwich grill, crêpe maker, or waffle iron are typically used only a short period of time and do not contribute significantly to your electric bill. However, if you are really inspired, there are easy, handy alternatives for all those electric appliances that use less power, or no power at all.

LIFE-CYCLE COSTING

When it comes time to replace an aging or worn-out appliance, try to look beyond the purchase price. You should also consider how much it will cost to use the appliance. Two appliances may have similar features, but consume different amounts of energy over their lifetimes. Comparing the life-cycle cost, or what it costs over its entire lifetime, is an easy and effective way to figure out which appliance is the most energy efficient.

Here's what you do. Estimate how long the appliance will last. Estimate the lifetime operating cost of the appliance. This usually includes both energy and maintenance costs. The yellow Energy Guide label will indicate the estimated annual energy costs. Finally, add the purchase price and the lifetime operating costs together to get the total life-cycle cost for the appliance.

Here's an example. Refrigerator 1 costs $600 to purchase and $100 a year for an estimated fifteen years. Therefore, its life-cycle cost will be $2,100. Refrigerator 2 costs $700 to purchase and $75 a year for fifteen years. Its life-cycle cost is $1,825. Therefore, even though Refrigerator 2 has a higher purchase price, it is a better overall investment.

CHAPTER 5

—— SOLVING HOT —— WATER PROBLEMS

Hot running water is one of the great inventions of modern civilization. Two hundred years ago only a minority of families in this country had indoor running water. One hundred years ago a minority had indoor hot running water. Today, most homes have both hot and cold running water at the turn of the tap.

Now water is becoming more scarce and expensive. Everywhere, hot water costs more and more. Fortunately, there are many easy ways to conserve water.

Hot water is important in three areas of the home: kitchen, bathroom, and laundry. They combine to make the water heater one of the major energy consumers in the home, whether your fuel is oil, gas, or electricity.

The hot water problem becomes entirely another matter when a switch is made to solar or other alternative-energy sources, and there are chapters on those matters for you to consider.

Let's say, though, that you're with the great majority: hot water is available at a twist of the wrist from at least three faucets (it's seven in our house), serving one or more major appliances, and brought up to temperature by your heating system or a separate hot water heater. You may well have bought this book because you know you have a hot water problem. You're aware of it every time you pay the bills.

By the standards of former times, we all live like kings. More and more, though, hot water at the fingertips demands increasing prices. This chapter is intended to help you scale down the use and cost of hot water.

These proposals can significantly alter the employment of hot water at your house, without uncomfortable sacrifice, and with resultant important savings. Let's get at it.

It's Dish-Washing Time

Yes, it's necessary to talk about washing dishes. The experts disagree on how hot the water should be in the household supply. Some say if you have an automatic dishwasher your water heater should be set at 150° F. Perhaps it should, if you have a need for something approaching sterilization. Otherwise, even with a dishwasher, 140° F. should be plenty hot enough. You can test it with a candy thermometer.

Is that temperature important? You bet. Heating water is the second greatest consumer of energy in the home, amounting to as much as 20 percent of the total domestic energy bill. Water being heated to more than 120° F. will need to be cooled again for almost all purposes, which is wasteful. Turn down the heater thermostat.

Whether you have a dishwasher, or do the dishes in the sink, an adequate supply of certain items will save fuel. You may not need two dozen pickle forks or three score demitasse cups, but it's a rare household that has too many spoons, coffee mugs, drinking glasses, or bowls. If you run short on these items constantly, buy an additional supply — maybe at the dime store — and you'll be running the hot water for dishwashing less often.

What is true for spoons and mugs is also true for saucepans and frying pans. Having some extras of these items will mean you run the hot water for cleaning a single item much less often.

With a dishwasher, letting dishes stack up till you have a full load every time is an important money saver. Grit your teeth and get used to it. Letting the dishes, pots, and pans pile up in the sink is much more economical than washing them a few at a time.

The most expensive way to rinse the dishes before putting them in the dishwasher is under a running hot-water faucet. Next most expensive is in a sinkful of hot water. Best is in a sinkful of unheated tap water. Perhaps not too pleasant, but entirely effective.

If plates are crusted with breakfast egg, or a pan has beans burned on the bottom, let the items soak for a few hours in unheated tap water. Nine times out of ten that will turn the trick at much less expense than a hot water soak, or scrubbing under a running faucet.

When shopping for a dishwasher, look for a model with a switch to cut off the automatic water heater and drying cycle. This will reduce energy consumption one-third to one-half.

You already have a dishwasher with that feature? Well, when you can, watch the cycle dial. When it gets to the last air-dry segment, just turn it to stop and open the door. In the winter a little extra heat and humidity will be added to the room by this process, and those dishes will dry by themselves quite quickly.

Utensils that are used regularly for nonstaining jobs like heating tea water don't need to be washed. They can be turned over in a sink rack and left to dry for the next use.

Incidentally, don't pour that hot water down the drain after boiling eggs or making spaghetti. Stopper the sink and leave the hot water in it for later washing chores, or just let it sit in the sink and cool. Letting the heat from the water radiate into the rooms makes more sense than heating a drain pipe.

Knives used for clean chores like cutting a grapefruit don't need the whole hot-water cleaning treatment. A quick splash under the cold water faucet and a wipe with a towel will do it. In fact, if you have good knives with riveted wooden handles, that cleaning method is much better for the knife than a hot-water soaking.

If you have an undersink garbage disposer, flush it with cold water. You'll not only save energy, but the cold water will solidify the greases, making them less likely to stick to the pipes and form a blockage.

USING THE BATHROOM

The invention of the single-action mixer faucets was a convenience breakthrough. But also a serious economy hazard. With that single-spout faucet you can get just the water temperature you want and let it run. Terrible. It would be better if you still had two separate faucets as your grandmother did. Then you'd need to stopper the sink and mix the right temperature in the bowl. Do it. You'll save money. With four people in the house, each one using the bathroom sink, say, five times a day, just filling the sink instead of letting the water run might save as much as forty gallons a day in hot water. That's enough for two full loads through the washing machine, or three quick showers.

That quick shower takes about half as much water as a tub bath. Call soaking in the tub an occasional luxury, and the quick shower a frequent sanitary necessity. A low-flow showerhead can reduce the hot water by as much as 50 percent. Most people won't feel a bit difference, or prefer them to their old showerheads.

When you take a tub bath, don't drain the water when you're through. Let the heat from the water radiate into the room until the water is cool. This, incidentally, is the basic principle of some of the solar heating systems. You might even stopper the tub when you take a shower, and let that hot water radiate its heat before it goes down the drain.

Be sure you turn off the faucet all the way when you're finished using sink or tub. If it still drips, ouch! One drop per second from a hot water faucet is 200 gallons a month, 2,400 gallons a year.

COLD WATER FOR YOUR LAUNDRY?

Consider the cold water detergents. Only clothes that are very greasy need water as warm as 80° F. to get clean. Your washing machine probably has setting for cold, warm, and hot water. Use the cold for ordinary washing, the warm for very dirty clothes, the hot not at all. Your wash-and-wear clothes made with synthetic fibers will be just as clean and considerably less wrinkled if you use cold water for washing. And by using cold water washing techniques you could save ten to fifteen dollars a month in hot water costs. With today's detergents, cold water rinsing is fully effective, and the rinse cycles are probably half of the water you use in washing.

Running your washing machine for just a few items? Wasteful. Perhaps it's because some of the necessary items in the household are in short supply, so you're washing more often than you need to. Stock up at least a week's supply of the commonplace, most-used items like socks and underwear. It's cheaper to have enough for each person so that use of the washing machine can be less frequent.

A larger supply of the frequently washed clothes will also allow better use of the different washing cycles with full loads. Lightweight items such as underclothes, handkerchiefs, blouses, and pillowcases can take a shorter cycle than heavyweights like blankets, jackets, and dirty towels. Have a sufficient supply so you can make up full, separate loads of the different kinds of washes you do.

WHAT ABOUT YOUR CLOTHES DRYER?

You've heard the lecture. Do complete loads. Use the most appropriate temperature setting. Keep the lint filter clean. And above all, when purchasing a clothes dryer, look for the model which uses the least energy.

You will need hotter temperatures for some things like baby clothes. Have enough of these, too, so you can make up full loads and make the most of the hot water you use.

When shopping for a new washing machine, look for the versatility of partial-load washing for those times when you'll need it, and for the ability to wash at different temperatures. Beyond that, be skeptical of over-fussy controls and multiple cycles. All that electronic gadgetry runs with electric current and spins the meter. Once you have figured out which features you need, select the model which uses the least energy.

SIX WAYS TO CUT HOT WATER COSTS

Here are six ways you can cut the costs of heating water in your home:

1. Locate the water heater as near as possible to the places where hot water is used. Water cools as it makes a long trip through pipes.

2. Insulate the hot-water pipes so they will retain more heat, particularly on those long runs of pipe.

3. Insulate the hot-water pipes that travel through unheated areas and cold cellars. Both pipe insulation and wraparound insulation can be bought at most hardware stores and is simple to install.

4. Pad the water heater with batts of six-inch fiberglass insulation that's used in ceilings. The cost of this will be about $10, and your savings will pay for it quickly.

5. If yours is an electric water heater, check with the power company about an off-peak meter. This means your heater will operate at times when the company has power to spare, and you can buy at a lower rate.

6. The water heater has a drain valve at the bottom. Use it about twice a year, or more often if there is considerable sediment in your water supply. Draining the heater will allow the heating elements to operate more efficiently.

CHAPTER 6
— - SAVE WITH SOLAR —

In the seventies many people assumed that by the turn of the century most new homes built in our country would be designed to make effective use of solar energy. Federal energy policies promoted solar energy and conservation, and provided tax credits for households which installed solar energy for heating or hot water. During this period, many existing homes were built or retrofitted with various kinds of solar energy devices. This momentum stalled somewhat during the eighties. Hopefully, we will make more progress in the nineties.

In any event, the move to solar energy has already begun. Today there are thousands of homes fitted with solar energy systems.

If a solar energy system is of interest to you, read on. There will be some ideas here you can use.

To start with, you're already using solar energy. The sunlight which comes in through every window adds to the heat in your home. Unfortunately, at night, your heated air leaves through these very same windows. That is why good draperies or insulating window shades are so effective.

The most light, and therefore heat, enters through your south-facing windows. That's why these windows are the most effective solar collectors. I'm not talking about some new development by which you can make your house look like a space station. I'm talking about plain, old-fashioned windows.

Sun heat is obviously present on every clear day. Not so obviously, the warmth of the sun is still with us on cloudy days. In fact, the hours of daylight even on a dim day have something to offer in reducing your fuel bills.

If you get intrigued with the solar possibilities, there are books and plans available that will take you beyond the scope of this chapter. We hope herein to offer some suggestions, some things you can do right away, at minimal cost and effort, to take greater advantage of that great free source of energy, the sun.

USE SOLAR HEAT — NOW

Don't think of solar heat as something for the future, in a new home. Make use of it now. Here are some ways to do it.

➡ Taking advantage of the sun's heat begins on the outside of your house. Black and other dark colors absorb sun warmth; white and light colors reflect that warmth. Assuming you live where it gets cold in the winter, dark colors for your house exterior, and particularly your roof, will pass through more of the available heat from the sun.

➡ You can get sunburned under water; you can get sunburned on a cloudy day; you can get sunburned through a T-shirt; you can get sunburned on a ski slope when the temperature is below zero. Naturally, the windows of your house, and especially those facing south, can pass through a lot of sun heat.

➡ Storm windows impede the passage of sunlight very little, but they do keep in more of the heat once it has entered your house.

  Most conventional greenhouses have glass on four sides with a glass roof as well. The plants get a lot of light. However, the heating bill is enormous. At night, the heat leaves through the glass walls and roof. A solar greenhouse usually has a large, sloped south-facing glass area receives the light the plants need to grow. However, the other sides are well insulated to reduce the heat loss to the outdoors.

➡ One of the concepts in use in complete solar energy systems is the heat collector. This is often a bed of sand or rocks under a house, or a large mass of water, in which the sun's heat can be stored. In a solar greenhouse, sun heat is stored in the soil and in water containers. At night, this heat radiates into the greenhouse and keeps it from getting too cold. You can take advantage of this concept by having solid objects standing in the sunlight to store warmth that will be radiated after the sun goes down.

➡ One good heat collector is a windowsill row of flowerpots, or an indoor windowbox. The earth in pots or box will store warmth during the day with the double advantage of helping the plants to grow and warming the room at night.

➡ Will the low-lying winter sun slant across the room to warm a brick-fronted fireplace, a slate entryway, or a similar solid surface? Be sure the draperies are pulled back to take advantage of this solar collector. Don't forget to shut them at night.

➡ Light-colored shades or slatted blinds drawn across a sunny window will reflect the sun warmth right back outdoors again. During the daylight hours, keep the sunny windows in the clear to let that sun warmth in.

➡ The first step for many people will be a solar hot water system. Such systems are now available either for new homes or for retrofitting on older homes. They will furnish from 50 to 100 percent of the hot water requirements. Look at your current cost to heat hot water and talk to a contractor to discuss the costs and savings. Ask your contractor for references so you can get an even better idea of how much your neighbors have saved from their solar hot water heaters.

➡ Are you on a tight budget? If you have unused space up under your roof — and this will certainly be true if yours is a newer house with a truss-roof design —

consult with a plumber on the cost of putting an old-style, secondhand, uninsulated hot water tank up there. Make sure your attic floor can support the added weight. At least during the warmer months, the upstairs tank, linked in the water lines before the water gets to your regular heater, will preheat the water, making less work and less fuel usage for household hot water.

➡ If your roof is insulated, rather than your attic floor, that up-top waste space will be warmer than the outdoors even in winter, so the tank up there can be an advantage in pre-warming your water all year-round.

➡ Sunshine is not only a source of warmth, but also, of course, a source of light at the same time. Flicking on the light switches in the daytime may be a habit you can break just by rearranging the furniture.

➡ Next time you're ready to repaint or repaper a room, think about how the room is used before you choose the colors. Light colors in a room will bounce the daylight around, making it a pleasant and cheerful place without extra illumination. This is a much less important factor in bedrooms, which are used primarily at night.

➡ In fact, in rooms used solely for sleeping the only advantage windows have is for a little ventilation. Wintertime solar heat just isn't available when the room is in use, so let the windows be small, or heavily draped.

➡ Window light in the kitchen is a tough problem, because you want a lot of storage, rather than windows, on the outside walls. Even more important, then, are the light colors for those kitchen walls.

➡ If you're designing from scratch, or doing a major remodeling, think about a combined kitchen-dining area with storage on the north wall and windows on south and east walls. That way you can have both storage and sunshine.

➡ Daytime reading and working areas can be placed where window light will be sufficient on all but the darkest, overcast days. Specifically, consider the location of the sewing machine, the chair with the magazine rack, the play table for the children, the workbench, as well as more obvious items like the artist's easel and the author's typewriter. Light also means heat, so you'll be warmer as you work.

➡ Are you planning to turn a dark attic into a bright living space? Installing a skylight is considerably less complicated and expensive than building a dormer, and will change a gloomy cave into a pleasant place. Make sure it is a high quality window or the heat loss in winter will much more than cancel out the savings you gain from the daylight. Look for a double-paned window with at least one-half-inch air space between each pane. Some skylights also come with low-e glass which makes them even more efficient. Finally, select the model with the lowest rate of infiltration. Don't forget about the insulated material to keep the heat in at night.

THE SOLAR ROOM

Some direct uses of solar energy are available to you.

Available to many homeowners is the sunspace or solar room — a considerable step ahead of the window greenhouse, but less expensive than a full-scale greenhouse.

➡ The solar room, of course, will do best if you build it on a south wall of your house. The next best choice is an east or west wall, depending on when you use the room and also how much the windows are obstructed by trees or neighboring buildings. It's best, of course, to have a minimum of shading in winter and some shading during summer to keep the space cool.

➡ Your solar room will gather heat even during overcast winter days. You'll have the most advantage from it when there are practical ways for you to conduct that heat to the rest of the house. Often a window or small fan will be sufficient to move the solar heat.

➡ There will be a natural daytime/nighttime temperature variation in your solar room, so grow the hardier plants and vegetables, avoiding the exotic tropicals that would require supplementary heat.

➡ Going to build a solar room? You'll have more advantage from it when the back wall is a dark color to absorb sun warmth.

➡ You'll add another dimension to your solar room benefits when the back wall is not only dark, but a solid masonry like concrete or stone that will retain sun heat into the nighttime hours.

Finally, don't forget the simplest solar energy device of them all, the solar clothes dryer. It works like a charm. It's also called the famous backyard rope clothesline, and it will save you about $50 a year.

CHAPTER 7

—— GOOD NEWS IN ——
YOUR GARDEN

Nationally, one of the major consumers of energy is agribusiness.

Once upon a time, food was raised with methods that the economists called "labor-intensive." Today, American food-raising is very clearly "energy-intensive." Petroleum-based herbicides, pesticides, and fertilizers are spread on the American farmlands by a variety of fascinating machines, including the crop-dusting airplanes. Planting, cultivating, and harvesting are all accomplished with more sophisticated machines.

Food products are processed in factories, refrigerated, trucked across the country, and then displayed in your supermarket, often in refrigerated cases. Every step of the way, energy is being consumed.

In fact, for almost everything you buy at the store, the fuel bill accounts for more of the price tag than the product itself. That's why growing your own fruits and vegetables can be a substantial money-saver.

Your own garden is "labor-intensive," in the manner of food-growing since the earliest days. The hand methods that are no longer practical on the commercial farms are still very effective in your backyard.

Just as you may have a power mower for your lawn, you may want a power tiller if your vegetable garden is of any size. This is a long way from the gallon-gulpers you see pictured on the big agri-spreads. Neither the mower nor the tiller is going to bankrupt you at the gas pump, particularly if you keep their engines tuned for efficient operation.

The secret to making your food garden a real money-saver isn't the growing of the food itself, it's in the preserving for year-round use on your table. An "eating garden" is mostly for fun and because you like fresh corn and tomatoes in season. The real saving is when you have nutritious, garden-grown edibles in the off seasons. Studies have shown that your garden can save more than $1,500 a year for a household of four.

Some practical food-preserving methods use no fuel at all, and other, sometimes easier, methods use little energy. Then there are the "energy-intensive" methods, like freezing. As in other aspects of your living, there are choices and compromises.

Food is one of life's necessities, not one of its options. At the market, $100 a week comes to more than $5,000 a year. Some of that market cost, for such items as pepper, matches, and toilet paper, will continue no matter how ingenious you are in your garden; and the miracles of modern science have yet to produce the pork chop tree. The estimate, though, that you can save about one-forth of that bill by food gardening at home is a modest projection.

Is the garden worth the effort? Since this is a book about saving money, that's a valid question.

Well, figuring a little less than a half-hour a day for thirteen weeks of the growing season, about ten hours to get ready and plant, about thirty hours to harvest and preserve, and a final six hours to put your garden to bed for the season, $1,500 worth of harvest is the equivalent of paying yourself about $16 an hour. You can decide if that's worth the effort.

MORE FROM YOUR GARDEN

Let's consider ways you can get more — and store more — from your garden.

The traditional rows of garden vegetables look very orderly and are well adapted to machine cultivation.

Actually, though, they demand a lot more work than is necessary. Many vegetables such as peas, beans, and leaf lettuce, do much better when planted in beds instead of in rows. Chard, spinach, beets, and carrots also take well to bed-planting instead of row-planting. The advantage is less time with the tiller because the beds require less cultivation through the growing season. And of course there's a great saving to space. Try a seedbed two to four feet wide. You'll soon learn how to sprinkle the seeds for proper spacing.

Beets and particularly carrots are very slow getting started. Mix some radish seeds in with each of these. The early radishes will mark the bed, and as you pull them up for eating they will make room for the carrots and beets.

When picking your harvest, do a little kitchen work before you go in the house. Corn husks, tops of radishes, and carrots, pea shucks and other throwaways can be left right in the garden plot. They will return to the soil and help to nourish it without artificial fertilizers. This is particularly important if you have been accustomed to grinding these things down the drain through the garbage disposal unit.

Save paper bags. When you go to the garden to harvest, take a recycled bag with you. Do the preliminary preparation there in the garden plot, and bring a bag of ready vegetables into the house.

When planning your garden, think of storing crops without wasting energy. Winter squash, onions, corn, carrots, turnips, parsnips, kidney beans, and potatoes all can be stored without canning or freezing.

DRYING AND STORING

Peel back the husks on ears of corn, but don't tear them off. Using about half the husks, break three ears together and hang them on the wall or in the attic. The kernels will dry, and can be renewed months later for eating by soaking them overnight in water or milk. The kernels taken from three good-sized ears will make a side dish for four at the table.

Dried corn can also be ground into cornmeal. Either soaked for serving, or fresh-ground for mush or baking, the dried corn is sweet and delicious.

Onions can be braided by their dried tops and hung to dry. When it's time to use them they'll be just like the ones you buy at the store, with dried layers on the outside and a tasty onion inside.

In the spring, dried onions are inclined to obey their natural impulses and start sprouting. Don't fight it. The first scallions will be along in the garden in a few weeks. The sprouting can be minimized by putting the onions in the refrigerator.

Winter squashes will store for as long as six months in a cool place, with no loss in flavor or nutrient value. Leave them outdoors in the fall to harden their skins before storing them. It's best to have them off the ground for that hardening process.

Where's a cool place? Old-time farm homes had what was called a **root cellar.** Often it was separate from the house, dug into an earth-bank, or set into a pit in the ground. You can set aside a corner of your cellar for a cool room, put up walls, and insulate them. There's a double advantage: You not only have a convenient, no-cost vegetable storage, but it's also a section of the house you don't need to pay to heat.

Potatoes, apples, pears, quinces, carrots, beets, parsnips, and turnips will store well in the cool room. Check with a good book on food preserving for the appropriate methods.

If underground, or well insulated in your cellar, your cool room will maintain a fairly constant 45° F. all year-round. That's about the same temperature as your refrigerator, which means it isn't suitable for long storage of meats, but will cool beverages to a pleasant chill for summer enjoyment.

Navy beans, lima beans, peas, and kidney beans can be dried easily for storage. Let them ripen on the vine and begin drying in the pod, then spread them on cloths (that's what you were saving that torn sheet for) to finish drying in the sun. When the drying process is complete, store in closed jars for later use.

Apple slices, carrot strips, and many other fruits and vegetables can be dried for storage. What you need is a book on food preserving.

Home dehydrators will speed up the drying process, and you may need one, considering how uncertain the sunshine can be at the end of the growing season. Look for maximum fuel economy. The models differ considerably in their fuel efficiency.

> The microwave can be used in a variety of ways to preserve and dry foods. Refer to your microwave instruction booklet or a microwave cookbook for safe instructions.

Efficient Ways to Can

After cool storage and drying, canning is the most energy-efficient. This has nothing to do with cans. Canning is putting up foods in glass jars, which must be sterilized by boiling. When you have a wood stove, you'll make out best in fuel efficiency, because you can bake in the oven and cook stovetop meals in the same cycle as your canning.

Canning efficiency is increased as your batches get bigger. Get a production line going, so that when one batch of jars and lids is sterilized, you're ready to use them and put in the next batch.

Canning is the most efficient way to keep tomatoes, the preferred way for pickles, and a good way for jams, jellies, and maple syrup, so learn the basics of the canning method.

Shelf space in a coolish place is mandatory for keeping the product of your canning efforts. That probably isn't on shelves over the refrigerator, where exhaust heat from the refrigerator motor creates extra warmth. See if there is room for shelves along the cellar stairs — the old-timer's favorite spot for canned goods — out in the garage, or in your cold room. Don't expose your canned goods to freezing temperatures.

If there is cupboard space in your kitchen for your supply of canned goods, let it be in an enclosed place where nothing else is stored. With the cupboard doors opened only for taking out foods at mealtimes, the space will stay cool, which is good for the canned goods, and also is one more chunk of space you don't need to pay to heat.

INDOOR GARDENING

Don't be satisfied with corn pone, dried beans, and jerky beef for those winter meals. An important part of the good news from your garden is that you can have a garden indoors for those salad greens.

Leaf lettuce is easy to grow in pots or windowsill boxes. Consider putting an extra-wide sill on one of your big south-facing windows, and filling the sill with edible plants. The humidity they will add to the room will be welcome in the winter, and they will give you salads every days while others are paying those high prices for long-distance lettuce.

Another expedient is to install a set of shelves across that south window, to increase your indoor garden growing room.

You can grow fresh spinach, chives, parsley and other herbs in windowsill pots or growing boxes. The flats you may use for starting bedding plants in the spring won't do for this purpose. The soil is too shallow for good root growth, and the shallow seedbed will be a nuisance for needing to be watered too often. Let your growing soil be as deep as you can manage conveniently.

Tomatoes and green peppers can be grown successfully in indoor pots. The little globes called cherry tomatoes are recommended. Both tomatoes and peppers require a substantial amount of soil for best growth — about a bucketful per plant, which suggests that one kind of pot to use is an ordinary bucket.

Red clay pots can be almost as big as buckets, and they are a bit more decorative. Don't try to hide these vegetables. Put them right out in the room by that sunny south window. As their fruits mature, they will provide a bright and colorful touch.

The tomato plants will need some help to pollinate and as the fruit matures. Use sections of broomstick jammed deep into the dirt to stake them up. When blossoms appear, tap the stems with one finger daily, to start the fruiting process. Strips of cloth for tying are less likely to bruise the stems than lengths of cord. Use colorful ribbons with big bows if you like to have fun in your house.

COLD FRAMES AND GREENHOUSES

More traditional for fresh vegetables in the winter is the outdoor cold frame, which in the older time was an unused glass storm window placed over a box sunk into the earth. Even in the northernmost states, you can count on salad greens for Thanksgiving dinner from a cold frame that has required almost no effort.

➡ A somewhat more elaborate application of the same principle is the sun-heated greenhouse developed by Scott and Helen Nearing. It furnished them with fresh vegetables right through the winter months.

➡ Yet another alternative is the window greenhouse, a cheery design whether or not you plan to grow vegetables. It provides many times the space of a windowsill, with the simplest kind of construction. There are commercial brands available for various sized windows; detailed plans can be purchased if you want to build it yourself. It's easy.

➡ Go the whole route. Build a solar room. You'll find it described in the chapter on solar energy.

➡ A separate greenhouse of commercial design, or even one attached to your house, may not give you a net energy saving. Heating one is expensive, and electrically operated temperature and humidity controls may run up the bill, too. Without those controls, you'd need to be in hourly attendance, adjusting shades, opening vents, and spraying mists.

CHAPTER 8

— WHAT YOU SHOULD —
KNOW ABOUT HEATING
WITH WOOD

As the prices for conventional fuels steadily rise, more and more people are considering the possibility of burning wood at home. Wood as a fuel source has advantages and disadvantages.

Advantage: Wood is considered to be a renewable resource. If we plant and harvest it wisely, we can keep using wood without using it up. Getting that down to personal terms, a well-managed woodlot no bigger than twelve acres will provide enough fuel for an average home, every year, forever.

Disadvantage: We know that in many parts of the world wood is extremely scarce. Poor planning and harvesting too frequently can deplete this vital natural resource.

Advantage: Wood as a source of heat can feel so good. It's toasty and homey to sit around a wood stove. After being outdoors on a cold day, nothing feels better than sitting next to a warming fire.

Disadvantage: Wood is not a very clean fuel. Wood smoke contains many pollutants which reduce the quality of the air we breathe. Many cities and towns now limit the number of households which can have wood stoves. If you're considering purchasing a wood stove, ask about emissions and efficiency. The catalytic stoves of the 1980s and 1990s burn much cleaner than the older models. More on this later.

If you have a fireplace, you no doubt enjoy a wood fire.

You need to know that a fireplace is an inefficient way to burn wood, and requires some managing just to give you a net heat gain. We'll explain that a little later. Even so, a fireplace is a start.

In fact, a fireplace can be a fine start, because it means you have a chimney available, which is one of the essentials for using wood as fuel. There are a number of good wood stove models that are designed to fit on your fireplace hearth and be vented up the fireplace chimney, so if you get at all serious about wood fuel, a fireplace can be a substantial beginning.

It can be helpful to know which are the better kinds of wood to burn. Locked in a hickory log, for instance, is twice as much potential heat as in a butternut log of exactly the same size. When looking for fuel efficiency, this kind of knowledge can be very helpful, and it's outlined in the pages that follows.

Much of the wood-burning wisdom goes back to the very dawn of civilization, because wood was the original fuel, and, in fact, was the dominant fuel in use in the United States as recently as 150 years ago. The tools, equipment, and know-how for using wood fuel are all readily available, both because there are many homes where wood has always been used for heating, and many more where the roofs are sprouting shiny new chimneys.

Incidentally, we don't plan to get into the details of wood stove installation and maintenance, which is the province of other volumes, but we feel compelled to offer one caution. By its very nature, an open fire in your home can be dangerous, and there are particular hazards inherent in the chimneys of fireplaces and wood stoves.

Before installing a stove get some expert advice, or at least start with an authoritative book on the subject. We'd hate to think that your reading of this chapter might create an enthusiasm that would place the safety of your home in jeopardy.

About any way you use wood as fuel, you're going to get some exercise. At the very least, you'll be carrying logs to the fireplace, or sticks to the stove, and later getting the ashes into a bucket or scuttle for removal. The exercise scale goes all the way from those modest chores to full management of a woodlot and felling your own trees. Where you want to be on that scale will depend on how much time you have and how much energy you have to give.

Every part of the wood fuel process you do yourself will save you money. Where I live, for instance, a cord of wood split, delivered, and stacked in yard or garage, will cost $75 to $100. It takes about seven cords to heat my house for the winter, so getting my fuel that way could cost $500 to $700, which would be cheaper than running the oil burner. However, I can cut it myself in the State Forest for a minimal fee, and I can cut it on my own land for nothing.

I have bought wood already split; I have bought wood ready for splitting; and I have cut my own. What I do depends in part on my available time when the woodpile needs replenishing. For a cheery fireplace, or a complete wood heat system, you'll likely make your decisions that same way.

Open up the damper and fire the kindling. Here we go.

A More Efficient Fireplace

You have a fireplace? Let's start there.

➡ A fireplace is likely to steal more heat than it delivers. The necessary draft up the chimney pulls warm air from the room, resulting in a net heat loss. This is particularly true as the fire is dying down, radiating less heat into the room, but still having a good draft up the chimney.

➡ Your fireplace should have a damper, a gate that closes off the chimney at the throat of the fireplace. As soon as a fire is out and no longer smoking, the damper should be closed. An open fireplace damper will drain heat from a house as fast as an open window.

➡ Glass doors on your fireplace will let you see the flames, while minimizing the heat loss from the room. They are particularly valuable after you've gone to bed, leaving a dying fire, because they cut off the heat loss from the room as the fire dies.

➡ Another compromise is the Franklin stove (which bears little resemblance to anything inventor Ben Franklin ever designed). You can open the cast-iron doors to enjoy the open fire, then close them at all other times to achieve something like a closed, cast-iron box stove.

➡ There are many makers of Franklin stoves, and some are better than others. The cheapest ones are likely to have a cast-iron front and top, and sheet metal sides and back. This is less desirable. A cast-iron model is best.

➡ Some of the Franklin models are designed to sit on your fireplace hearth and be vented up the fireplace chimney. A worthwhile idea. Some models have an additional door on the side for firing the stove while the front doors are shut. Some also have an interior baffle system for greater fuel efficiency.

➡ If you're planning to build an open fireplace, consider including a sheet metal Heatilator box. It will draw in cool air from the floor, warm it around the firebox, and send it warm into the room from vents. By combining it with a glass screen, you can have a modicum of heating efficiency this way.

➡ Another fireplace accessory is the hollow-tube grate. This is a set of metal pipes open at both ends, used instead of andirons. The pipes are shaped with their lower ends facing the room near floor level. The pipes run back across the bottom of the fireplace, and up the back of the firebox, with the upper ends aimed out into the room again. As the fire heats, a draft is created in the pipes, picking up cooler air at floor level, warming it, and sending it back to the room as warm air. Some of the models are augmented with an electric blower. You can decide for yourself whether you like the way it looks.

➡ The greatest heat loss from a fireplace may be during the night, after an evening fire, when the damper must remain open to let out the smoke. Covering the fireplace opening with a sheet of asbestos millboard or aluminum will cut off this flow of heated air up the chimney.

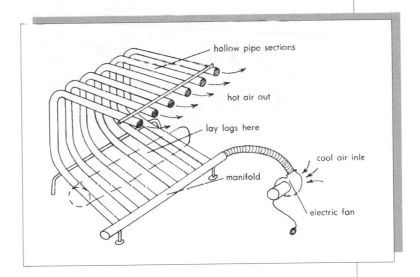

hollow pipe sections

hot air out

lay logs here

cool air inlet

manifold

electric fan

SPEAKING OF WOOD

Let's talk about wood.

The accompanying charts show the actual fuel values in various types of wood. The differences are significant. In some areas the fuel woods of lesser value are more readily available, and everywhere pine is easier to cut and split than beech. Get acquainted with what burns best and longest among the woods available where you live.

Here's a diagram describing the actual dimensions of that mysterious measurement, the cord. Because so many homeowners don't know that a full cord is 4' x 4' x 8', the woodseller can often get away with selling what he loosely calls a cord of wood that is really precisely what he felt like throwing on the truck that day. Knowing can be saving.

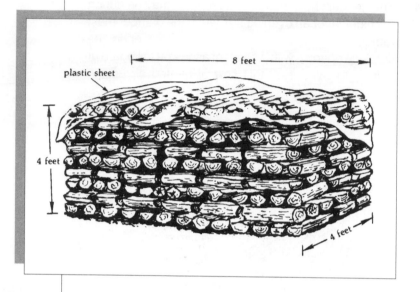

Burning fresh-cut wood will deposit creosote in your chimney that can result in a chimney fire. You'll run less risk and need to clean your chimney less often if you always burn wood that has been cut and split at least six months.

You can be sure you're burning dry wood when your home supply is stacked at least six months before you intend to use it.

Stacking wood in the side yard? Put down parallel poles with the bark still on and stack on top of them. Eventually they will rot, but that's better than having the ground rot eat away firewood into which you've put the work of cutting and splitting.

Split Your Own Wood

➡ Think about buying your firewood unsplit. It will be less expensive that way. Good exercise, too.

➡ Splitting wood on the concrete floor in cellar or garage, or on a brick or stone hearth, is a sure way to ruin your axe, no matter how careful you think you can be.

➡ Some woods don't split worth a darn. Birch and maple split beautifully. A piece of gnarled cherry is tough one. Choose your firewoods with this in mind if you're going to do the splitting.

➡ Don't try to split long sections of wood before cutting them into stove or fireplace lengths. Do the cutting first. Short lengths split much more easily.

➡ For splitting firewood, a somewhat dull axe is better than one with a razor edge. There's not only less risk of cutting yourself, but also less chance of getting the axe stuck in the wood.

➡ Hold the axe handle as near to the end as you can comfortably, and take a full swing. That way the momentum weight of the axe-head will be doing the work, instead of just your muscle power.

➡ You'll want an axe whose head tapers out to a flat wedge. A slender head is more likely to get stuck in the log. A double-bitted axe with two blades is designed for another purpose entirely. It is dangerous to use and too slender for best splitting.

➡ For splitting big, knotty lengths of wood, a maul or a sledgehammer and some splitting wedges will do the trick. A maul looks like a sledge with one side tapered to an edge. Splitting wedges look like fat slices of pie made from tempered steel.

➡ If you're going to get into splitting a year's supply of fuel wood for your home, consider a power log-splitter. You can probably get one at the tool rental shop in your town for $25 to 40 a day. Follow directions carefully.

➡ If you have a big, fat stump in your woodpile that looks as if it isn't going to split easily, don't bother trying. That's just the one you need for a chopping block. You've got two? Take the extra into the house for a stool by the fireplace.

➡ For sawing trees or full-length cordwood into burning lengths, a chain saw will be fastest. Among the hand tools, a bow saw or a bucksaw are best. Cutting firewood with a carpenter's handsaw will wear you out, and chopping it to length with an axe is something you should try only if your doctor recommends an excess of violent exercise.

➡ Even the best of us miss a stroke now and then when splitting wood. Don't ignore those chips. Gather them up for starter kindling.

➡ Birch logs are pretty just as they are sawed from the tree, but they must be split promptly. Birchbark is almost completely waterproof (the native Americans made canoes from birchbark) and unless you split it, the inside wood will rot quickly and get "punky," rendering it useless for firewood.

All of what has just been said about preparing wood for burning applies to stoves as much as it does to fireplaces, and a good wood stove is many times more fuel-efficient than a fireplace at its best.

THE HELPFUL WOOD STOVE

Here are some handy wood-stove thoughts.

When choosing a wood stove, consider one with a flat top where a pot of water can simmer during the day. It will add needed humidity to your room, and will be ready for cups of tea or coffee without starting up the cooking range.

Like other appliances, some wood stoves burn wood more efficiently than others. Your stove's workmanship and design are important features which affect efficiency. Make sure your new wood stove has a catalytic combustor. This increases the efficiency and reduces the pollutants it sends into our air. Many stoves are now tested and rated for seasonal and combustion efficiency. Compare efficiencies when purchasing this major appliance. And remember to make sure your stove is correctly sized for the space it will need to heat.

If you'll be using an older stove, look into installing a catalytic add-on to increase efficiency and reduce emissions of your stove. With a wood stove in your plans, consider a wood-burning cookstove. Some of the models are very attractive, and all have the advantage of saving on kitchen fuel as well as providing room heat.

When starting a stove fire, use rolled paper, slender sticks of kindling, and one or two pieces of split wood. Open all the drafts, get a good fire going, and add more wood when your "starter set" has become a bed of coals. Then adjust the drafts and add more wood as needed when each firing has been reduced to hot coals.

In a well-made, cast-iron wood stove, some sticks just smouldering on a bed of hot coals still put out a lot of good warmth, and they'll quickly spring to a blaze even after several hours, as soon as you open the drafts and add a little oxygen from the outside.

A wood stove is most efficient when installed near the center of the house, on the first floor, or down cellar.

A stove in the cellar will help to keep the water pipes from freezing in a winter emergency.

You can always start a stove fire with paper and well-split kindling. If you can't, then check for blockage in your stovepipe draft. Do not use lighter fluid, gasoline, or other such flammables to start an indoor stove fire.

You can burn rolled newspapers in your wood stove. One stick of firewood with each two "newspaper logs" makes a good combination, and is a lot better than paying to have the old papers recycled.

Coal burns much hotter than wood. If you burn coal in a stove designed for wood, you may overheat the grates and cause them to have a ruinous warp. Yes, you can even open the drafts on a wood fire and get it so hot it will warp the grates and even warp the top of your stove. This is most likely to happen when you're trying to get a wood stove hot too fast. Take it easy. Your stove will get up to best heat in due time. Don't try to force it.

If you are using a wood stove regularly, two woodboxes are a good idea; a larger one for the day's fuel supply, and a smaller one to hold kindling splints. Neither woodbox should touch any part of the stove. That dry wood ignites very easily. Keep it thirty-six inches from the stove.

There's a temptation to use your wood stove as a trash disposer. The best recommendation is — don't. It's an unnecessarily risky way to try to save money. In a fireplace or stove, paper trash and other flash flammables like Christmas tree branchesburn too hot, and with big flames that can cause a chimney fire. Recycling your paper trash is a much better idea. Artificial logs made of pressed sawdust impregnated with wax, or other artificial compounds can also be dangerous. If a fire gets out of control for any reason, the artificial logs are almost impossible to extinguish.

A brick wall behind your stove will not only make it safer to operate, but will also hold and radiate heat, multiplying your stove's advantages. **Careful.** Bricks one at a time may not seem to be particularly heavy, but even a modest brick wall can weigh several hundred pounds. Be sure your floor is well enough braced underneath to carry the load of wall plus stove.

When you have a wood stove, give your trash a second look. Anything wood will burn, and broken, unusable furniture is almost always good dry hardwood.

Someone taking down a dead tree in the neighborhood

may create an opportunity for you when you have a wood stove. Check with the tree crew. Any part of the leftovers they'll put in your yard, or let you haul away, can be either kindling or firewood.

FOR SAFER, EASIER WOOD-BURNING

Here are some ideas that may make your wood-burning easier as well as safer.

➡ Don't exhaust a wood stove into a flue already in use. Each fire must have a flue of its own.

➡ Insulated, double wall stovepipe is your best bet for an outside chimney. There will be less moisture condensation than with a single-wall pipe, and therefore less buildup of the flammable carbons and tars that cause chimney fires.

➡ A heat exchanger for your wood stove flue pipe will increase the heat output. There are several designs, all calculated to extract heat from the pipe before the smoke gets outdoors. Some have an electric fan to blow the trapped warmth into the room.

A few final thoughts on heating with wood:

➡ Maybe your house design will allow a small access hatch between the woodpile and the location of your stove or fireplace. That will eliminate carrying wood in from the outdoors, which resultant opening and closing of doors.

➡ A light mist of water sprayed on the ashes in stove or fireplace before you remove them will minimize the "fly ash" spreading around the room. Recycle one of the "spritz" bottles to turn the trick, after it is emptied and well rinsed of its window cleaner, deodorant, or kitchen spray.

Choosing Firewood

1. The Good Woods

Tree	BTUs per cord in (000s)
Shagbark Hickory	24,600
Black Locust	24,600
Ironwood (Hardhack)	24,100
Apple	23,877
Rock Elm	23,488
White Oak	22,700
Beech	21,800
Yellow Birch	21,300
Sugar Maple	21,300
Red Oak	21,300
White Ash	20,000

2. Second-Choice Woods

Tree	BTU's per cord (in 000s)
Black Walnut	19,500
White Birch	18,900
Black Cherry	18,770
Tamarack (Larch)	18,650
Red Maple	18,600
Green Ash	18,360
Pitch Pine	17,970
Sycamore	17,950
Black Ash	17,300
American Elm	17,200
Silver Maple	17,000

3. Hardly Worthwhile Cutting

Tree	BTUs per cord (in 000s)
Red Spruce	13,632
Hemlock	13,500
Black Willow	13,206
Butternut	12,800
Red Pine	12,765
Aspen (poplar)	12,500
White Pine	12,022
Basswood	11,700
Balsam Fir	11,282

CHAPTER 9
— SOME OLD-TIMER'S — WISDOM

It wasn't so long ago when spun-glass insulation had not been invented, automatic oil burners were still in the future, and triple-track aluminum storm windows hadn't even been thought about. Those days were like today, though, in that people wanted to be comfortable at home in the wintertime.

Lacking many of the innovations of modern technology that we take for granted, they applied their ingenuity to keeping warm and happy while the wind howled around the corners.

We can be no less ingenious in our own time. In fact, there is considerable overlap between yesterday and today. Many of the ideas in this chapter are drawn from the lives of present-day country people who still practice the arts of their forebears. Why? Because the old ways still work.

Some of the ideas may strike you as quaint, corny, and impractical. Then there will be the one that strikes you with the ring of reason and you'll try

THE BEST BOOKCASES

My maternal grandfather was a scholar and teacher, so naturally he had a lot of books. His bookcases had sliding glass doors, which offered a double advantage. With the doors closed his books didn't get dusty — and dusting books is a miserable chore. The second advantage was that with the doors closed the bookcases were closed space that didn't need to be heated.

it. And that will be justification enough both for my having written it and your having read it.

There is no intention here to present an exhaustive encyclopedia of pioneer arts. Rather, the intention is to pique your imagination into some new ways of thinking. The ideas here — many of them — are quite individual. The ways in one household were not necessarily the ways in another, because the people were different; and even the houses were different and in their shapes suggested different expedients.

You're different, too, and your house and its living patterns is not exactly like any other on earth. Consider these ideas, then, not only as things you can do, but as guides to a way of thinking.

You might also consider some conversation with the oldest members of your family. They'll be pleased that you want to learn from them, and you may hear some great old stories with nuggets of wisdom tucked away in them. The old-timers knew how to have a pretty good life without the advantages and appliances we have. Check it out.

YESTERDAY'S IDEAS FOR TODAY

Here are some of the old-timers' ideas for keeping warm.

➡ Consider the humble footstool. Its real purpose was to get your feet up off the floor where the coolest drafts were swirling around. Place a footstool at each comfortable chair in the living room and you might be able to turn down the thermostat by several degrees.

➡ Keeping your ankles warm contributes greatly to keeping your whole self comfortable. That was the idea behind gaiters, spats, and other ankle-warmers. Try heavy slipper socks for each member of the family to wear in the evening. The kind with leather feet will last longer. Just those warm socks may let you notch down the thermostat a degree or two.

➡ Another ankle-warmer is tucking a throw rug at the base of each door leading to the outdoors. Even a hardwood doorsill will wear, and then the chills seep through when the wind blows.

➡ Another way to combat the floor chills is to bank the foundation of the house. Raw dirt used for banking will eventually rot out the wooden sills, but loose straw worked well in the older times, and hay bales or bagged leaves are often used in the country today.

➡ You can often identify an older house by the chimney rising through the middle of the roof. The chimney at the end of the house may have some aesthetic appeal, but most of the warmth it holds will be wasted on the

BED WARMERS

We lived out past the end of the power lines for awhile when I was young, so winter warmth was achieved old-style. Each of us kids had a good-sized round stone as a personal possession. (You could use a brick.) Each night our stones were heated in the oven of the kitchen range, then my mother would wrap each one in soft flannel and put it in the foot of the bed. Nothing quite like that warm, flannel-wrapped stone to greet your toes as you push down through the cool sheets.

outdoors. That central chimney spread all the warmth it could before the smoke got out.

➡ At the turn of the century a mark of elegance and luxury was to have high ceilings in the downstairs rooms. It meant you were so wealthy you could afford to heat that extra overhead space. The high ceilings still feel good.

But if you have one of those older homes and if fuel bills get too high, you might consider installing a drop ceiling, at least down to the tops of the windows. It isn't hard to do and will save considerable on fuel bills. However, in order for this to be effective, you will need to make sure any bypasses have been sealed. If you insulate above the drop ceiling you will save energy and add a degree of noise-proofing to the room.

➡ If dropping the ceiling seems extreme, install a ceiling fan. It will serve to circulate the warm air back down to the living space.

➡ Lighting the individual places where people are reading or working will be less expensive than lighting a whole room with a ceiling light.

➡ In former times, people carried their lights with them as they traveled from room to room in the evening, instead of having the whole house lighted. The traveling light was most often a candle in a holder with a handle, or perhaps an oil lamp.

➡ When your back is warm, you're likely to feel warmer all over. That's probably why the vest and the sleeveless sweater were invented. If you buy or make one of these, be sure it's long enough to keep you covered when you bend over or lift your arms.

➡ Another traditional body-warmer is the afghan. Originally this was a small rug from Afghanistan, and later the term came to be applied to different designs of small blankets knitted or crocheted at home. Each well-equipped home had at least one afghan, draped over the end of the couch in the living room. It wasn't just a decoration. It was used for keeping the legs warm.

➡ You may have noticed that many of the old four-poster beds were perched on long, sturdy legs rather high off the floor. Well, the closer you get to the ceiling, the warmer it is. There was a practical purpose in that design.

➡ Three or four blankets get terribly heavy during the night. One alternative is the electric blanket, but it keeps the meter running. The old-timers counted on the down-filled comforter to keep them warm.

➡ The coverlet or bedspread on George Washington's bed was probably more than just a decorative item or a dustcover. It was likely a closely-woven, hand-loomed cover made of linsey-woolsey — a mixture of linen and wool. It's a warm combination, particularly when paired with that down comforter.

➡ Another old-time favorite was the bed-warmer — a covered, shallow brass pan with a long handle. Hot coals from the fire were put in the pan, then it was passed between the sheets just before bedtime. Delightful. The brass bed warmer also worked for roasting chestnuts, and later generations have used it for making popcorn.

➡ Many of the older homes have a piece of furniture you might not be able to identify. It's a combination mitten warmer and towel rack. Small enough to be moved easily to just the right distance from the stove, it would dry out soggy mittens, have warm towels ready for the bath (what a luxury!), and even line up the boots to dry. It was made from pine planks and discarded broomstick handles — not a fancy item, but nifty. You could make one, and it would be worth its small effort if for nothing more than those warm towels.

➡ Today, almost all the shutters you see are purely decorative. Yesterday, they were part of the heating and cooling system. They would be closed on cold winter nights, and those on the sunny side would be closed to keep out sun heat on hot summer days.

➡ That big country kitchen was a homey place. In the winter, it was also the warmest place in the house, so it made sense that the kitchen was big enough for the whole family. With a lamp on the kitchen table, everyone would gather around the light in the warm room to finish homework, read, play games, or just munch on fresh cookies and chat.

➡ Many older homes had a summer kitchen added to the back of the house. It had a stove, a sink, and some storage space so cooking could be carried on without heating up the main house. The sink had a drain, but no running water, so there were no pipes to freeze in the winter. Off season, the summer kitchen was used as an unheated storage room.

➡ The old wood-fired kitchen ranges often had a warming oven at eye level. The flue pipe passed through it to give it a moderate temperature. Breads, muffins, rolls, and pies were popped inyo the warming oven for a little time before serving, and often the dinner plates were warmed there, too — a custom now practiced in the finest and most expensive restaurants.

➡ A cousin to the man's necktie and the woman's fashionable scarf — both relatively useless items of apparel — is that snuggly old item, the shawl. Girls knitted them; grandmothers crocheted them for

grandchildren; almost everybody wore them, both indoors and out. They were a most handy way to put on a little extra warmth around the neck and shoulders: less cumbersome than a jacket, less likely to muss the hair than a sweater. They were often made of light wool yarns in neutral colors such as grey, tan, and light blue that would harmonize with almost anything. A favorite shawl was a lifetime treasure. Usually wider and lighter in weight than what we would call a scarf, the shawl deserves a revival.

HOMEMADE ICE CREAM

The most eagerly anticipated summertime treat at our house when I was young was homemade ice cream. It was worth the effort of cranking the dasher for the delicious result. There are now electric ice cream makers, and mixes that will make a cold something in the freezer compartment of your refrigerator, but nothing will match the product of that old hand-cranked model. Try it with fresh peaches or fresh strawberries in the mix. Super!

CHAPTER 10
— KEEPING YOUR CAR —
HEALTHY AND EFFICIENT

If there is one reality that immediately identifies American society, it is the automobile. Not only has the horse and buggy disappeared, but the passenger railroad train has almost followed the trolley car down the tracks to nowhere. We're hooked on personal transportation in the form of that wonder of the modern world, the private motorcar. Regrettably, automobiles are large contributors of carbon monoxide and nitrous oxide to our atmosphere. These gasses contribute to the greenhouse effect and air pollution. Because it would be unrealistic to think that the automobile will be abandoned anytime soon, we need to find ways to use our automobiles more efficiently.

If you're this far along it's assumed you have a car or two, so you already know about the upward spiral in the cost of petroleum products. You've considered, or are already driving, a more compact vehicle to economize at the gas pump.

There are some basic principles that can be stated.

Your car isn't only toting you from here to there, it's toting itself. The less weight the engine must haul around, the more efficiently it will perform. Therefore, the smaller and lighter the car you can comfortably drive, the less it will cost to operate. Some auto manufacturers have gotten this message, but we still have a long way to go. In the meantime, shop for the most efficient car with the features you need.

The fewer the horses you have to feed to get you from here to there, the less it will cost. The big twelve- and sixteen-cylinder yachts on wheels that were the luxury cars of a generation ago aren't even available today unless you have one custom-built, in which case you probably aren't reading this book. They revved up a lot of horsepower that wasn't needed.

CHECK YOUR DRIVING HABITS

Your driving habits are a key to economical operation of your car. The place to begin understanding those habits is with a miles-per-gallon record that will take the guesswork out of driving economy.

The first place to apply that mpg record is in the regular trips you make, such as driving to work. You may be following a traffic flow, or going by what you think is the shortest way, but that may not be the cheapest route. If there are alternative ways from home to job, or any other regular destination, take the trouble to check them out for mileage efficiency. You may wind up going a new way.

The reason an alternative route may be less costly is that you car operates most efficiently at a steady speed. If the shorter route has lots of stops and starts it probably will burn more gas than a longer way around that lets you keep an even pace.

The other way to get there may have fewer stoplights. Good. With your engine idling you'll burn a gallon of gas in fifty minutes, going nowhere. Lots of zero-miles-per-gallon waiting at traffic lights and stop signs can be expensive over the course of a year. Have the right change

KNOW HOW TO START YOUR CAR

On some of the newer cars you dont have to step on the gas pedal before you start the car. If you must pump the gas pedal several times, something is wrong— have a mechanic look at it.

ready at toll booths on your way for minimum waiting time.

The most economical driving in any car is when you are just feeding enough gas to maintain momentum at a steady speed on the level. Build up that momentum in as relaxed a way as you can, consistent with the traffic flow. That means easy starts away from your driveway, away from the traffic lights — every time you are accelerating.

Remember, every time you touch the brakes you are paying to reduce the momentum that cost so much to build up. Watch the traffic signs and ease off gradually instead of having to use your brakes to get to a slower speed.

Tailgating — driving too close to the guy in front — puts your driving pace at the mercy of his whims. As a tailgater you'll be alternately braking and pumping gas as you respond to the forward driver's perception of the road, which is different from yours. Tailgating is not only hazardous, it's expensive.

A quick jab at the gas pedal, or pumping the pedal, squirts raw gas into the engine's combustion system. Trying to get started, you can flood your engine that way, as you have probably already discovered. A smooth, steady pressure on the gas pedal is always a money-saver.

When you're approaching an uphill climb, there's a money-saving technique to use. Build up a little extra momentum as you approach the base, then keep it steady or even ease off a little as you are climbing. Trying to add speed as you are climbing a hill is one of the most expensive maneuvers you can devise. It you're driving a low-horsepower car uphill, be prepared to downshift rather than feed more gas in high gear. It's cheaper.

If you have a choice when you are traveling, make your stops on a downhill slope. Starting from scratch is much cheaper when you're rolling downhill.

Resist the temptation to coast on a long downhill. In

many states this practice is illegal, and for good reasons: it's dangerous. When coasting, you don't have the control of your car that is possible with the engine engaged. Your brakes can overheat and fade away; you run the hazard of locking your steering wheel in some cars, and you'll save very little gas. When going downhill leave the engine engaged, but take your foot off the gas, or touch the pedal oh-so-lightly.

Ease off on the speed. A car that gets 40 miles per gallon at 40 miles an hour might get as little as 25 miles per

MAKE A LIST

We live about twenty-five miles from town, so we make lists before we go shopping.

It's a pain in the neck to get back home and discover we've forgotten something. The household shopping list is an excellent idea. It not only cuts down the number of shopping trips, but also makes each trip one that can be planned for minimum mileage.

We find that the combination trip is useful. We combine going to church in town with a visit with some friends and relations; schedule a trip to the dentist together with shopping, buying postage stamps, and getting the dog to the vet. Some household cooperation gets more accomplished with minimum mileage.

gallon at 70. A ten-mile trip flat-out at 60 will take ten minutes. I will only take two minutes longer at 50, and that kind of difference can be blown away at a stoplight, or looking for a place to park.

Either with air conditioning in the summer, or with the heater in the winter, the natural flow of air makes using the blower fan unnecessary at over 40 miles per hour. Since the fan itself can subtract as much as one mile per gallon to operate, that's something to consider, particularly on a long trip.

In the winter, start off slowly in a cold car. All the lubricants are like molasses for a mile or two. They'll loosen up, and then your engine won't need to work so hard to keep you moving at highway speed. A short warm-up of the engine before starting can also help reduce engine wear, since the first ten minutes are the hardest-wearing — especially in cold weather.

How to Stretch a Tank of Gas

You can get six to twenty percent better mpg with a properly tuned engine. Keeping a mileage record will tell you when your mpg is slipping, which is a signal for a tune-up.

➡ There are a few items you can take care of easily without going to a service station. One of them is the air filter. A clogged air filter leaves your engine gasping for breath and means you're probably running with a "rich" mixture, that is, more gas and less air. Many chain and auto stores carry air filters and they are simple to change. A clogged air filter can cost you one mpg. Fix it.

➡ Dirty oil cuts back engine efficiency. You can change your own, and buying your own oil is much cheaper than getting it at a gas station. There's a drain plug under your engine that will come out readily with a wrench. Have a bucket ready to catch the dirty oil. Remember to return the used oil or dispose of it safely.

If your fan belt is too tight, your engine is working too hard and wasting gas. The belt should give a little to finger pressure when the engine is not running. If it doesn't, the adjustment is easy to make with a wrench.

➡ Badly worn spark plugs can cost you as much as two mpg. You'll need a special wrench to remove the spark plugs for inspection, and when you get them out you may not know a good one from a bad one. This is probably a job for a trained technician. If you decide to check the plugs yourself, be sure you mark the leads to the distributor cap before taking them off the plugs, so you can get them back on in the proper order.

CHECK YOUR TIRES

Let's take a look at the tires.

Your owner's manual has important information on your tires, including the air pressure that should be in them. Underinflation of your tires can cost you as much as one mile per gallon; overinflation will wear the tires out sooner. You can buy a small pressure gauge and check the pressure yourself from time to time more accurately than the reading on the gas station airpump.

Radial tires have 50 percent less road resistance, and so they give you from 3 to 19 percent better miles per gallon. They also wear about three times as long, so they're a good buy even though they are expensive.

Radial snow tires also have less road resistance than conventional winter shoes, while still giving necessary road traction.

➡ The plugs may need just a little elementary cleaning you can do by scraping with a jackknife blade. If one of the plugs looks very different from the others — it's very oily, or blacker, or badly pitted — you have a situation that calls for a trained mechanic.

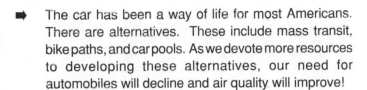

- The car has been a way of life for most Americans. There are alternatives. These include mass transit, bike paths, and car pools. As we devote more resources to developing these alternatives, our need for automobiles will decline and air quality will improve!

- Heavier cars are more costly to run. A reduction of 200 pounds in automotive weight typically improves fuel economy by nearly 5 percent.

- Use the car air conditioner as little as possible. The air conditioner uses a lot of gas.

- Using cruise control can save gas. If you drive on the open road often, staying at a constant speed can save fuel.

- If you are taking a trip, start early in the day while traffic is light. Plan to stop for meals at times when traffic is heavy.

- Do not let your car idle for a long time to warm it up. Also, don't let your car idle for more than a minute after it is warmed up—it wastes more gas than restarting your car.

- Do not rev the engine and then quickly shut your car off. This wastes gas. It also pumps raw gasoline into the cylinder walls. This can wash away a film of oil that protects the cylinders. This will increase engine wear.

- The good news is that in the United States during the past 15 years, the average car's consumption of fuel has fallen by 50% due primarily to the more fuel-efficient automobiles.

- More good news is that emissions of major urban pollutants have dropped substancially, the result of more complete combustion of fuel and the catalytic conversion of carbon monoxide, nitrogen oxides, and hydrocarbons into carbon dioxide, nitrogen, and water.

CHAPTER 11
—YOUR NEXT HOUSE—

The average American family moves from one home to another every five years. Considering that group of people who settle down and stay as a part of that average, most of us move fairly often.

With that thought in mind, it seemed worthwhile to consider some of the factors you might have in mind when you're looking for your next house. Maybe you'll be building from scratch; maybe you'll be shopping for a house someone else built, but either way you can look for advantages that wouldn't be practical to build into your present home.

You'll probably get closest to the ideal if you're in a position to build from the ground up, so much of this chapter makes that assumption. Even if that's not your situation, you can be looking for the home you would build if you could.

Often, successful living is the art of compromise. You'll be weighing one set of criteria against another set, and deciding where the compromises must be made. In general, remember that investments in energy conservation result in decreased operating costs. Therefore, even if an energy efficient house costs more to build or to buy, the monthly mortgage payment may be the same or lower. And you will be a lot more comfortable in an energy efficient home.

And, when looking for a new home, you can be making mental assessments as to the feasibility of modifications and adaptations that will make daily living more practical. Moving the structure to another position on the land may be impossible. Insulating the walls or attic is easy and inexpensive in many situations.

Let's assume our search is in an area where the seasons include cold winter months.

STUDY THE HOME'S SETTING

If you're looking at home sites in a hilly area, the best location is on a southeast slope. A little rise to the west will tend to cut the force of the prevailing winds in winter, and the southern exposure will both take maximum advantage of the southern sun for winter heating, and give the best prospects for gardening in the summer.

Having picked an ideal location, you will be best off if the principal windows face south, and the structure is positioned on an east-west axis to provide a south-facing roof. Deep overhanging eaves on the south side will let you take maximum advantage of the winter sunlight, while shading you from the direct heat of the summer sun.

Broad-leafed trees on the south side of your house will make a cooling shade in the summer, then conveniently drop their leaves and let the winter sun warmth through, just when you want it.

A solid windbreak of hardy evergreens to the west of your house, and some more on the north side, will be a welcome shield from the winter winds, and will break the sunbeams in the heat of the late afternoon in summer.

A light-colored roof will reflect heat; a dark-colored roof will absorb heat. With a truss roof and extra space above the ceiling, that roof color factor won't make a lot of difference. If there is usable space under the roof and adequate ventilation available, the dark-roof option will save money during the winter months.

Small windows on the north side will provide summer cross-ventilation and minimum exposure to winter cold. Be sure those north windows are double-glazed, or covered with storm windows. Low-e glass or argon-filled windows will reduce the heat that is lost through your windows even more.

A CLOSE LOOK AT THE HOUSE

If the grounds satisfy you, it's time to study the house itself — closely.

The two-story design is far more economical than the extended single-floor plan. The principal heat loss in a house is through the walls and roof, so the less surface area you have, the less it will cost to heat.

Who you select to build your home may be the most significant decision you make. Try to find a builder who is informed about the latest developments in energy-efficient new home construction. Your discussions should include how the house will be framed; how much insulation will be installed in the walls, attic, foundation, basement ceiling; type of windows which will be installed; choice of heating systems; and airtight construction. The more you know, the better your house will turn out.

If you are building your own home, definitely use 2x6s instead of the usual 2x4s in framing outside walls. This will permit the use of a heavier layer of insulation. A bonus advantage is an interesting window option; you can set your windows flush with the outer wall and give yourself deep windowsills indoors, or you can do the opposite for an unusual deep-set window effect from the outside.

Building an airtight home is easier than trying to tighten an existing home. A state-of-the-art home, from the energy perspective will have extremely low infiltration rates. The builder will use special techniques to install a continuous vapor barrier on the interior walls and ceilings. It will be important for the electrician and plumber to understand the importance of sealing the holes they make. The builder will use a blower door to make sure the house is sealed and tight. At this point, you may want or need to install mechanical ventilation. This will ensure adequate ventilation levels in every room. Moisture from the kitchen and bathrooms will be vented to the outdoors.

One of the major decisions you will may need to make in building your home is what kind of heating system to install. Because your heating system should last about thirty years, this presents a good opportunity to invest in energy conservation. Make sure you compare the installation and operating costs for each system. For example, electric heat is relatively inexpensive to install, but more expensive to operate than oil or gas. Select an energy-efficient heating system. There are many improvements in this technology. For example, new oil- and gas-fired systems vent directly to the outdoors and, therefore, no longer need chimneys.

There are numerous features which will affect the home's overall energy consumption. A house that is planned for energy saving will have an unheated garage, woodshed, or toolshed shielding a west or north wall. The buffer space of those unheated rooms is excellent insulation.

Many contemporary designs locate closets and other storage spaces in the house interior, because they don't need the windows that are associated with outer walls. The center of the house, though, will be the warmest place in winter, and not the most sensible place for storage. Try

YEAR-ROUND COMFORT

The wing we built on the schoolhouse is half below grade and we located three bedrooms there. Their windows are smaller and higher up the wall than they might otherwise be, but since bedrooms are used primarily at night, the size and placement of windows isn't critical. The downstairs bedrooms are easy to heat in winter, and stay cool for summer sleeping.

for a design that puts closets and storage spaces on north and west outer walls, where they can serve as insulators.

Functions that require plumbing will be clustered: that is, the kitchen, bath, and laundry will be as close to each other as possible. This is easier in a two-story design. That way the water and drain lines will be short (which will save money for openers if you're doing the installing), making them easier to secure in a wintertime heating emergency. Also, short hot water lines keep the water warmer between heater and faucet.

Rooms that may be unused in winter should not have water lines running through them. Given the absence of water lines, extra rooms with separate thermostats can be shut off when they are not in use. There's a money-saver.

Consider getting along without general, full-room illumination for evenings. The wall switches at the room, entry can be wired to plug outlets where individual lamps can be positioned.

Where full-room illumination is indicated, as, perhaps, kitchen or playroom, get acquainted with the varieties of fluorescent fixtures. The cool tubes use just one-fourth the power of incandescent light bulbs, and are available in warm color tones that are much easier on the eyes than they used to be.

When buying or building, give a thought to chimney placement. The central chimney will radiate warmth whenever the heating unit is in use. If you are planning to use one or more wood stoves, be sure your house design allows for easy chimney placement.

A final consideration:

You may not want to build or buy a solar home now, but will the design of the house you are thinking about adapt to solar installation at a later date? It's called retrofitting. If the principal roof area is facing south, you're on the way to a solar water heater, and then complete solar heat.

CHAPTER 12

——— TIPS FOR AN ———
ENERGY-EFFICIENT
APARTMENT OR
CONDOMINUM

Approximately 22 percent of the energy used in the United States is consumed in residences. Most of the energy consumed in apartment buildings still comes either directly or indirectly from fossil fuels: oil, natural gas, or coal. These fuels are nonrenewable resources. In the case of oil and natural gas, world supplies could be exhausted in the forseeable future. Therefore, it is in everyone's best interest to use these precious resources wisely while new energy sources are being developed.

Despite major successes in energy conservation in the last decade, there is much that Americans can still do in this area. This chapter contains information on a number of measures that will help you reduce the amount of energy you use in your apartment, house, or condominium, while also making it a more comfortable place to live. Some of the measures suggested may seem trivial, but when added to those that you and others already employ, the result can be significant in energy savings for our nation.

These energy conservation measures are largely no-cost, low-cost (under $10), or moderate-cost ($11 to $50); even the most expensive would probably cost well under a $100 to implement. Few of the measures require any significant physical alterations. Most require only a change in your energy use habits.

Nationwide, space heating is the largest consumer of energy in residences, and accounts for nearly 50 percent of energy used in a typical household. Water heating accounts for 14 percent, refrigeration for 13 percent, space cooling for 7 percent, and lighting, cooking, and appliances account for the remainder.

This chapter suggests ways you can seal up leaks in your apartment so that heat doesn't escape in the winter and cool air doesn't escape in the summer. It will tell you how you can turn down your thermostat in the winter and turn it up for summer cooling while maintaining a comfortable living environment.

It will show you how you can reduce the total wattage of lighting in your apartment while increasing the amount of usable light. It outlines steps you can take to reduce the amount of hot water you use for bathing, dish-washing, and laundering, and how to make the most energy-efficient use of your appliances.

Caution. Persons over 65, infants, and persons with certain illnesses risk hypothermia if they stay indoors at temperatures under 65° F. If you think you risk hypothermia by turning your thermostat below 65° F., consult your doctor.

HEATING

The Biggest Energy Consumer. Nationwide, more energy is consumed to heat apartments and houses than for any other purpose, so the largest energy savings can be made in this area. (Note: in some areas of the southern United States air conditioning or water heating may account for a larger share of regional energy consumption.)

➡ Thermostats. For apartments that have them, thermostats offer the single easiest opportunity to conserve energy, requiring nothing more than setting a dial to the desired temperature. Advice on settings range from 65° F. to 68° F. for the hours you're active and 50° F. to 60° F. when you're in bed.

➡ Setback Features. Some thermostats have an automatic setback feature that can lower the temperature around the time you go to bed and raise it again shortly before you get up. More complicated thermostats provide for double setbacks, allowing you not only to automatically reset the temperature at night and in the morning, but to automatically lower it during the day while you're out and raise it shortly before you return in the evening.

Although many people mistakenly believe that it takes more energy to heat up a cold apartment than it does to keep it at a constant comfortable temperature, this is *not* the case. In many cold climates, for each degree you can set your thermostat back for twenty-four, hours you will save about three percent on your heating bill.

➡ Avoid Drafts. Make sure your thermostat is not in a draft. It will sense the cooler air and make the furnace work longer overheating your apartment.

➡ Radiator Tips. If your apartment has radiators they should be kept clean, since dirt and dust absorb heat. Radiator covers should be removed when radiators are in use because the covers absorb heat and block the flow of air through the radiator.

➡ Radiator Types. There are two types of radiators: steam and hot water. In general you should adjust your radiator's steam or hot-water valve only to turn it on or off. Positioning the valve in between does not regulate heat, but only strains the pipes. If your apartment is too hot, don't open the window. Instead turn the valve all the way off until the temperature in your apartment is comfortable.

➡ Bleed Radiators. To operate most efficiently, a hot-water type radiator must be completely filled with water.

At least once a year at the start of the heating season your radiators should be purged of trapped air. Do this by opening the bleeder valve on each radiator. The bleeder valve is the small valve located at the top and on the end of the radiator. Some bleeder valves can be opened with a screwdriver while others are opened with a key available at hardware stores. When the valve is opened, any trapped air will escape with a hiss followed by a flow of hot water. Once water begins to escape close the valve immediately. Throughout the heating season, bleed radiators that are running cooler than normal.

➡ Air Vent Valves. If your apartment is equipped with steam-type radiators it is important to check their air vent valves each heating season. This vent allows air to escape so that steam can enter the radiator. The valve is usually a small chrome-plated device mounted on the top of the radiator at the end opposite the steam valve. This valve should always be standing straight up with the vent hole at the top. The vent hole must be kept free of dirt and paint for the radiator to operate efficiently.

➡ Radiator Reflectors. Radiator reflectors are usually made from a thin bubble-pack material with aluminum or another shiny substance on one side. Placed on the wall behind the radiator unit, they reflect heat back into the room, instead of allowing the heat to seep through the wall or nearby window. They are a moderate-cost item available from hardware stores.

➡ Build it Yourself. You'll spend even less money if you build your own reflector. Obtain a piece of cardboard or insulation board and cut it to cover an area of wall slightly larger than that covered by the radiator. Cover one side of the board with aluminum foil or some other reflective material. Then fasten the reflector to the wall behind the radiator. Whether you buy or build a reflector, be sure that when installed it does not touch the radiator, since it will conduct heat into the wall behind it instead of reflecting it back into the room.

➡ Doors. Your apartment will lose warm air to an unheated hallway or to the outdoors, so keep your apartment door closed.

➡ Weatherproofing Doors. A poorly fitted apartment door will allow warm air to escape from an apartment during the winter months. However, there are a number of simple no-cost or moderate-cost techniques for making your door more airtight. Warm air can escape between the door frame and the wall. If this is the case in your apartment, caulk between the frame and the wall.

➡ Door Sweep. The loss of warm air is frequently greatest under the bottom of the door. This air loss can be prevented by installing a door sweep on the bottom edge of your door.

➡ Draft Guard. A no-cost or low-cost alternative to a door sweep is a draft guard. This is a sand-filled tube of cloth which is laid against the bottom of your door. You can buy this product cheaply, but the no-cost way is to make it yourself. Cut a four-inch to five-inch wide strip from an old sheet, dress, or shirt. The strip should be several inches longer than the gap it will plug. Sew the sides and one end together. Then fill with sand and sew shut. Around the remainder of the door, weather-strip where the door closes against the frame.

➡ Windows. During the winter months pull shut blinds, shades, and draperies on all windows at night and on windows with a northern exposure during the day. Open them on windows whenever the windows receive direct, warming sunlight. Uncover east-facing windows in the morning, west-facing windows in the afternoon and windows with a southern exposure during all daylight hours.

➡ Weatherproofing Windows. There are a number of ways that warm air can escape through you windows.

It can leak out between the window frame and the wall. This type of leak can be stopped by caulking between the frame and the wall.

➡ Leaky Sashes. Warm air can be lost between the movable window sash and window frame, and between the top and bottom sash in a double-hung window. (The window sash is the panes of glass and framework into which they are set.) In this case, air loss can be prevented by weather-stripping the movable sash.

➡ Using Caulk. Rope caulk can be placed over the cracks between the sash and the window frame, and where the upper and lower sashes meet. Most people only use rope caulk for one season ,although it can be removed, rolled back up, and stored in a jar until next year. A disadvantage of rope caulk is that it must be removed in order to open the window.

➡ Types of Weatherstripping. Plastic, adhesive weatherstripping can be placed on the window frame, pressing it against the sash. This type of weatherstripping will last longer than rope caulk, and the window can be used without removing the weatherstripping.

The most durable type is the extruded plastic or V-strip that can be placed between the sash and the frame and between the upper and lower sash. Typically, this weatherstripping will last for several years and does not interfere with the use of the window.

➡ Loose Panes. Air can also escape around the edges of a loose pane. Caulk or tape around the edge of a loose pane where it meets the framework of the sash. If you have a cracked pane of glass, you can find out if it is losing heat by holding a stick of burning incense up to it. Is the smoke drawn out the crack? If so, replace the cracked pane, or tape over the crack until the pane can be replaced. Weatherproofing your door and windows will make your apartment more comfortable while conserving energy.

➡ Inexpensive Storm Windows. During the winter months a great deal of heat is lost through the glass in your windows. Ideally, your apartment is supplied with storm windows, but if not you can purchase inexpensive storm window kits or make your own out of clear plastic sheeting. The sheeting is applied to the inside of the window frame and completely covers the sash. The plastic will stop leaks, and the dead air between it and the window will slow the transfer of heat to the outside.

➡ Buying Plastic Sheeting. The plastic you will use can be purchased by the roll. It should be at least eight mils thick so that it's rugged enough to last the entire winter. Buy it wide enough to cover your widest window outside of its frame from one side to the other. Estimate the length of plastic you will need by measuring the height of each of your windows from the bottom to the top of their frames and adding their total height.

➡ Applying Plastic Sheeting. There are a number of methods you can use to apply the plastic to the window frame. These include tape, glue, tacks, and wood strips and nails. No matter how you apply it, for maximum effectiveness make sure that the seal between the plastic and the window frame is airtight. Leave one or two windows free of plastic so they can be opened for ventilation.

➡ Air Conditioner Covers. Window- and wall-mounted air conditioners cool your apartment even in winter by letting in chilly drafts and by presenting a cold surface. If you can't remove the unit and close the window, this energy loss can be stopped with an outdoor air conditioner cover made of tough plastic. An inside cover should be used in addition to or (if you cannot safely reach the outside of your unit) in place of an outdoor cover. Air conditioner covers are low-cost items.

➡ Exhaust Fans. When not in use, a kitchen exhaust fan allows warm air to escape from your apartment. Low cost covers are available for exhaust fan openings.

➡ **Furniture Arrangement.** Arrange your furniture and draperies so they do not block or obstruct heat vents, radiators, air conditioners, or baseboard heaters.

AIR CONDITIONING

➡ **Air Conditioner Cleaning.** If you use a room unit in your apartment check the filter at least once at the beginning of the cooling season. If it's clogged, your unit will operate inefficiently and run longer than necessary. Clean the filter or replace it — it's a low cost item. If you can do so safely, check and clean the condenser coils and fins (the grills or spines on the outdoor side of the unit).

➡ **Temperature Control Setting.** The temperature control should be set no lower than 78° F. Most window units do not have specific degree markings, so refer to a thermometer placed in a part of the room away from the unit's air flow. Don't set the control to a temperature below 78° F. when starting up the unit. It won't cool the room faster, and if you forget to set it to a higher temperature once the room is comfortable, you'll be wasting energy.

➡ **Air Conditioner Thermostat.** Don't place lamps, TV sets or other heat sources near your air conditioner thermostat. Heat from these appliances is sensed by the thermostat and could cause the air conditioner to run longer than necessary.

➡ **Buying a Room Air Conditioner.** Check the Seasonal Energy Efficiency Rating (SEER) and select the model with the highest number to obtain the greatest energy efficiency. Make sure the unit you purchase is not too big for the space you need to cool. An oversized unit won't cool your house properly. Instead you will spend more money to be less comfortable than with an appropriately sized unit.

➡ **Dress Cool.** Wear loose, lightweight, light-colored clothing in warm weather. This type of clothing allows air to pass across your skin evaporating moisture and cooling you.

➡ **Window Fans.** The outdoor air temperature is frequently comfortable, especially at night, but there may be no breeze to bring the cooler air into your apartment. Buy an outdoor thermometer, a low-cost item, and mount it so it's visible from your window. It will tell you when it's cool outside. When the temperature outside is comfortable, use a window fan instead of continuing to use the air conditioner. A fan requires as little as one-tenth the energy needed to run an air conditioner.

➡ **Fresh Air.** If your air conditioner has an outside air control to bring in fresh air, use it without turning on the cooling section. The compressor motor in the unit is the big energy user, not the fan. Be sure to close the outside air control when operating the compressor (cooling position) so that the compressor is cooling only room air.

Lights, Cooking, and Appliances. In the summer, electric lights, cooking, and the use of appliances such as the washer and dryer generate heat and increase the load on your air conditioner. Fortunately, the days are longer and we tend to turn on lights later. Keep lights low or off whenever possible. Try to schedule cooking and the use of appliances for the cooler parts of the day, i.e., the morning and late evening. If you must use the oven for a number of hours, shut the kitchen off from the rest of the apartment and use the kitchen exhaust fan to draw off the heat you create in cooking.

➡ **Humidity.** High humidity makes warm air even more uncomfortable, especially when you're active. Reschedule chores that produce moisture, such as floor washing, dish-washing, laundering, bathing, and showering until cooler times of day or night.

LIGHTING

➡ **Switch Habits.** When leaving a room for even a short time, turn off the lights

➡ **Use Daylight.** When possible, schedule those activities requiring good lighting for the daytime. Place your reading chair near the window. Dirty windows let in less light, so keep them clean.

➡ **Clean Bulbs and Fixtures.** Dirt and grime from cooking, cigarette smoke, and dust obstruct light, so keep bulbs, fixtures, and shades clean. For safety's sake remove bulbs from their fixtures before cleaning them and dry them thoroughly before replacing. Make sure bulbs are cool before cleaning. a hot bulb should never be put in water.

➡ **Lamp Location.** Make sure that lamps are positioned so that the most efficient use can be made of their light. If you have a lamp by your reading chair or at your desk, you won't have to light up the whole room.

➡ **Lamp Shades.** Many decorative lamp shades bottle up light or direct it where you don't need it. Light-colored translucent shades are the best for releasing light. Shades on reading lamps should direct most of the light downward. Remember to keep shades clean to let out more light.

➡ **Light-Colored Walls and Furnishings.** Lighter-colored walls, furnishings, curtains, and rugs reflect light and reduce the amount of artificial light needed in a room.

➡ **Reduce the Wattage of Light Bulbs.** The total wattage of light bulbs used in an apartment can be reduced three ways:

1. by using lower-wattage incandescent light bulbs
2. by replacing a number of lower wattage bulbs with one higher-wattage bulb
3. by replacing high-use incandescent bulbs with fluorescents.

- Lower-wattage bulbs should be used in halls, vestibules, and other places where no close-up work or reading occur. Energy-saving bulbs can be used to replace higher-wattage bulbs, often without a difference in lighting levels. The customary 40-, 60-, 75-, 100- and 150-watt bulbs are replaced by energy-saving bulbs of 34, 52, 67, 90 and 135 watts respectively.

- In areas that need better lighting it is generally more efficient to use a higher-wattage bulb than a number of lower-wattage bulbs. For example, you need six 25-watt bulbs to get the same amount of light you get from one 100-watt bulb, and the six 25-watt bulbs use 50 percent more electricity.

- Fluorescent Lighting. These use about one-quarter to one-fifth the amount of electricity as their incandescent counterparts do. For example, a 15-watt fluorescent bulb produces as much light as a 60-watt incandescent bulb. Even though the initial cost is greater, each fluorescent light will typically save from $40 to $70 in energy costs. It will also last about 10,000 hours or ten to fifteen times longer than incandescent bulbs. Any light which is on more than three hours a day is a good candidate for replacement.

  This technology is improving rapidly. The light is warmer and more pleasing. The flickering many people remember is no longer noticeable. More and more products are available which means you can find the right one for most situations.

- Safety Lights. Do you leave your lights on when going on vacation? Substitute compact fluorescents in these fixtures which will be on 24 hours a day.

- Correct Wattage. Have you installed the appropriate wattage for the task at hand? Lots of time bulbs with higher than needed wattage are used just because one runs out of the desired wattage bulb. For example, a lamp with a 75-watt bulb might provide suitable light with a 60-watt bulb.

→ **Task Lamps.** Task lamps provide direct lighting over desks, workbenches, sewing tables, etc. You save energy when you use them instead of the higher-wattage general lighting in the room.

→ **Long-Life Bulbs.** Long-life incandescent bulbs are more expensive and less efficient than standard bulbs of the same wattage.

→ **Dimmers.** Solid state dimmers allow you to reduce the energy going to incandescent bulbs. A light can be adjusted from bright for reading to a gentle glow for watching TV or dining. Some dimmers require no installation. The lamp is simply plugged into the dimmer and the dimmer into a wall socket. Wall switches can also be replaced by dimmer switches.

→ **Timers.** If you don't like coming home to a dark apartment, or want the added protection of leaving some lights on when no one's home, consider lighting timers, which turn lights on and off automatically at preset times. Using timers is much less costly in the long run than leaving your lights on all day.

WATER

→ **Water-Saver Shower Heads.** Water-saver shower heads cut the flow of water by 40 to 60 percent and typically have a water cutoff lever. With this latter feature you can turn off the water while you lather up. These shower heads frequently have settings for different types of spray. Water-saver shower heads are low-cost items that just screw onto your existing shower arm.

→ **Aerators.** Installing an aerator in your kitchen or bathroom sink faucet will reduce the amount of water in the flow. You'll use less hot water and save the energy that would be required to heat it. The sinks in many modern apartments are already equipped with aerators, so check with your landlord before trying to install one.

Appliances — General Tips

➡ Turn Them Off. Don't leave appliances running when you're not using them.

➡ Keep Appliances in Good Working Order. They will last longer, operate more efficiently, and use less energy.

➡ Be Energy-Conscious When Buying Appliances. Compare energy use information and operating costs of similar models by the same and different manufacturers. An appliance with a lower purchase price may in the long run cost you more than an energy-efficient model with a higher purchase price. Many types of appliances are required by law to have labels showing estimated annual operating costs. Find out if your utility company has any information or rebates to assist you in selecting the most efficient appliance.

➡ Special Features. Before buying a new appliance with special features, find out how much energy it uses in comparison to a model without the features. For example, a frost-free refrigerator uses more energy than one that must be defrosted manually. It also cost more to purchase. The energy and dollars you can save may make it worth passing up the convenience of such special features.

➡ Use Appliances Wisely. Use the appliance that requires the least amount of energy for the job. For example, toasting bread in the oven takes three times as much energy as toasting it in a toaster.

Refrigerator-Freezer

➡ A Major Energy User. Unlike most household appliances that are operated only periodically, the refrigerator-freezer operates 24 hours a day, 365 days a year. New York City estimates that over 25 percent of the general electrical costs in an average city apartment is accounted for by the refrigerator.

➡ Clean Coils. At least once a year carefully clean the condenser coils of your refrigerator, using either the crevice tool attachment of the vacuum cleaner or a long-handled brush. These coils are located either behind or beneath the refrigerator.

➡ Door Gasket. The gasket is the strip of flexible plastic or rubber around your refrigerator door that seals the crack between the door and the cabinet when the door is closed. Dried food on the gasket can break this seal, so clean the gasket periodically to assure that the seal is airtight.

➡ Temperature Settings. A temperature of 38° F. to 40°F. is generally recommended for refrigerators and 10°F. for freezers. Follow the manufacturer's instructions, but check these settings by placing a thermometer in both sections.

➡ Contents Arrangement. Food retains cold better than air, so keep units as full as possible but don't overcrowd so air can circulate freely. For the freezer compartment, stack items tightly. Add extra bags of ice if you don't have enough food packages.

➡ Humidity or Power-Saver Switch. Many refrigerators have a humidity or power-saver switch. Its purpose is to control small electric heaters around the edge of the door that stop the door from sweating on humid days. At all other times this heating serves no useful purpose. Keep it switched to the power-saving or low-humidity position for most of the year.

➡ Manual Defrost. Frost buildup increases the amount of energy needed to cool refrigerators and freezers, so defrost regularly. Never allow your freezer to build up frost more than one-quarter inch thick.

RANGE AND OVEN

➡ See the tips in Chapter 4.

- Cooking Tips. Use a steamer or pressure cooker if you have one. They not only save energy but also preserve the nutritional value of food.

- Burners. If you have a gas range, make sure the flame is blue and cone-shaped by keeping the burner clean and unclogged. You can use a piece of wire or pipe cleaner to unclog burner ports. If cleaning doesn't help, call your apartment superintendent or appliance service representative. Keep burner reflectors shiny and they will reflect more heat.

- Pots and Pans. Use flat-bottomed pots and pans, they provide faster heat transfer. The pot or pan should completely cover the burner or heating element. A small pan on a large burner wastes energy. Shiny pans and clean reflectors help focus heat.

- Turn Off the Range. If you use an electric range, turn off burners shortly before the recommended cooking time is completed. The heat retained in the element will finish the job.

- Lids On. Food cooks faster in pots and pans with tight fitting covers.

- Oven Habits. Plan to cook as many dishes together as possible. If one dish calls for 325°, another for 350° and a third for 375°, set the oven for 350°. Cut a few minutes off the recipe time for the lower-temperature dish and add a few minutes to the higher temperature dish.

- Don't Preheat. Preheat only when absolutely necessary and don't preheat for dishes cooked for an hour or more. In any case, never preheat for more than ten minutes.

- Don't Open the Door. Every time you open the oven door, the oven loses about 20 percent of its heat, so don't keep opening the door to see if your dish is done. Follow the time in the recipe instead.

➡ Don't Overcook. Use thermometers and timers to avoid overcooking.

➡ Small Ovens. If you have more than one oven, use the smallest one that will do the job. For example, a toaster-oven may cost half as much to operate as a full oven, but will cook or heat small items just as well.

➡ Use the Range Instead of the Oven. Whenever you can, use the rangetop instead of the oven. The range uses far less energy.

➡ Use a crockpot instead of the oven or range. It uses heat efficiently and costs less. Invest in a slow cooker and a cookbook, you'll be amazed at the variety of dishes you can make

➡ Double Recipes. When cooking or baking, double recipes and freeze half for future use.

➡ Frozen Foods. Thaw frozen foods (except when package instructions or recipes indicate otherwise) before cooking in the oven. Frozen meats require 20 minutes longer per pound to cook than thawed meat.

➡ Turn Off the Oven. Turn off the oven a few minutes before the recommended cooking time. The retained heat will finish the job.

➡ Oven Arrangement. Rearrange oven shelves before you cook, not while the oven is on. Allow at least one inch of space around each utensil in the oven and when using more than one shelf, stagger the utensils for better heat distribution.

➡ Minimize the Use of the Self-Clean Feature. Use the self-cleaning feature only when absolutely necessary. Start the cleaning cycle after using the oven to utilize retained heat. Wipe up oven spills regularly to avoid the need for frequent cleanings.

➡ No Foil. Never place aluminum foil on an oven bottom. It may block vents and impair air circulation, reducing

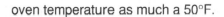

oven temperature as much a 50°F.

➡ Microwave Ovens. Microwave cooking is much more energy efficient than conventional cooking.

WASHER AND DRYER

➡ See tips in Chapter 5.

➡ Detergent. Use only as much detergent as recommended on the box. Excessive suds hamper effective washing and often require extra rinsing.

➡ Pre-Soak. Presoak heavily soiled clothing, or use the washing machine's soak cycle to avoid second washes.

➡ Don't Overdry. Overdrying wastes energy, sets wrinkles, and causes clothes to wear out more quickly. If your dryer has an automatic dry cycle, use it to prevent overdrying.

➡ Dryer Venting. Generally, dryers should be vented to the outside to avoid putting excess moisture into your apartment. However, if you have a dry apartment and an electric dryer, you may be able to vent the dryer into your apartment during winter. This will help heat the apartment and add moisture. Cover the vent with a nylon stocking or buy an indoor dryer-vent kit to prevent lint from escaping into your living area.

➡ Separate Clothes by Weight. Separate loads into heavy and lightweight items since the lighter ones takes less drying time.

➡ Dry Consecutive Loads. Drying your clothes in consecutive loads saves the energy required to warm the dryer up to the desired temperature.

DISHWASHER

➡ Full Load. Wait until you have a full load before you use your dishwasher, but be careful not to overload it.

➡ Scrape, Don't Rinse. Instead of rinsing your dishes in

hot water before loading them into the dishwasher, scrape them with a sponge or spatula.

➡ Rinse Hold Setting. Don't use the rinse hold setting on your machine. It uses three to seven gallons of hot water each time you use it.

➡ Air Dry. Some dishwasher models have an automatic air-dry or overnight dry switch. If yours doesn't, turn off the control knob after the final rinse then open the door and let the dishes dry by themselves. This can save you up to ten percent of your total dishwashing energy costs.

➡ Hand Dishwashing. Rinse your dishes in a sink or dishpan of clean rinse water instead of under hot running water.

OTHER APPLIANCES

➡ Garbage Disposal. Use only cold water when running your disposal. This saves hot water and solidifies grease which is then ground up and washed down the drain.

➡ Iron. An iron heats up much faster than it cools, so it saves money to begin by ironing low-temperature fabrics first then working up to those that require the highest temperature. Turn off the iron about five minutes before you complete your ironing and use the heat retained in the plate to finish the job.

➡ There are a number of ways you can reduce your ironing load. By promptly removing laundry from the dryer and either hanging it up or carefully folding it, you can reduce or eliminate the need for ironing. Hang clothes in the bathroom when you're bathing or showering — the steam will often remove wrinkles for you. Buy permanent press fabrics and garments.

➡ Hair Dryer. Towel- and air-dry your hair whenever

possible. Running an electric hair dryer for ten minutes uses the same amount of energy as burning a 60-watt light bulb for three hours.

➡ Television. "Instant-on" TV sets use energy even when the screen is dark. This type of set often has a "vacation switch" feature. If not, plug your set into a switched socket or have your TV repair man install an additional on-off switch in the cord or in the set itself.

➡ Water bed. Keep it covered during the day with a heavy blanket and insulate the sides at bottom. This way it will lose less heat and cost less to heat.